# Grantseeker's Toolkit

**Nonprofit Law, Finance, and Management Series**

*The Art of Planned Giving: Understanding Donors and the Culture of Giving* by Douglas E. White
*Beyond Fund Raising: New Strategies for Nonprofit Investment and Innovation* by Kay Grace
*Charity Advocacy, and the Law* by Bruce R. Hopkins
*The Complete Guide to Nonprofit Management* by Smith, Bucklin & Associates
*Critical Issues in Fund Raising* edited by Dwight Burlingame
*Developing Affordable Housing: A Practical Guide for Nonprofit Organizations* by Bennett L. Hecht
*Financial and Accounting Guide for Not-for-Profit Organizations, Fifth Edition* by Malvern J. Gross, Jr., Richard F. Larkin, Roger S. Bruttomesso, John J. McNally, Price Waterhouse LLP
*Financial Management for Nonprofit Organizations* by Jo Ann Hankin, Alan Seidner and John Zeitlow
*Financial Planning for Nonprofit Organizations* by Jody Blazek
*Fund-Raising: Evaluating and Managing the Fund Development Process* by James M. Greenfield
*Fund-Raising Fundamentals: A Guide to Annual Giving for Professionals and Volunteers* by James M. Greenfield
*Fund-Raising Fundamentals: A State-by-State Handbook of Registration Forms, Requirements, and Procedures* by Seth Perlman and Betsy Hills Bush
*Grantseeker's Toolkit: A Comprehensive Guide to Finding Funding* by Cheryl C. New and James A. Quick
*Intermediate Sanctions: Curbing Nonprofit Abuse* by Bruce R. Hopkins and D. Benson Tesdahl
*International Guide to Nonprofit Law* by Lester A. Salamon and Stefan Toepler & Associates
*The Law of Fund-Raising, Second Edition* by Bruce R. Hopkins
*The Law of Tax-Exempt Healthcare Organizations* by Thomas K. Hyatt and Bruce R. Hopkins
*The Law of Tax-Exempt Organizations, Sixth Edition* by Bruce R. Hopkins
*The Legal Answer Book for Nonprofit Organizations* by Bruce R. Hopkins
*A Legal Guide to Starting and Managing a Nonprofit Organization, Second Edition* by Bruce R. Hopkins
*Managing Affordable Housing: A Practical Guide to Creating Stable Communities* by Bennett L. Hecht, Local Initiatives Support Corporation, and James Stockard
*Nonprofit Boards: Roles, Responsibilities, and Performance* by Diane J. Duca
*Nonprofit Compensation and Benefits Practices* by Applied Research and Development Institute International, Inc.
*The Nonprofit Counsel* by Bruce R. Hopkins
*The Nonprofit Guide to the Internet* by Robbin Zeff
*The Nonprofit Law Dictionary* by Bruce R. Hopkins
*Nonprofit Litigation: A Practical Guide with Forms and Checklists* by Steve Backmann
*The Nonprofit Handbook, Second Edition: Volume I—Management* by Tracy Daniel Connors
*The Nonprofit Handbook, Second Edition: Volume II—Fund Raising* by Jim Greenfield
*The Nonprofit Manager's Resource Dictionary* by Ronald A. Landskroner
*Nonprofit Organizations' Business Forms: Disk Edition* by John Wiley & Sons, Inc.
*Partnerships and Joint Ventures Involving Tax-Exempt Organizations* by Michael I. Sanders
*Planned Giving: Management, Marketing, and Law* by Ronald R. Jordan and Katelyn L. Quynn
*Private Foundations: Tax Law and Compliance* by Bruce R. Hopkins and Jody Blazek
*Program Related Investments: A Technical Manual for Foundations* by Christie I. Baxter
*Reengineering Your Nonprofit Organization: A Guide to Strategic Transformation* by Alceste T. Pappas
*Reinventing the University: Managing and Financing Institutions of Higher Education* by Sandra L. Johnson and Sean C. Rush, Coopers & Lybrand, L.L.P.
*Strategic Planning for Nonprofit Organizations: A Practical Guide and Workbook* by Michael Allison and Jude Kaye, Support Center for Nonprofit Management
*Streetsmart Financial Basics for Nonprofit Managers* by Thomas A. McLaughlin
*A Streetsmart Guide to Nonprofit Mergers and Networks* by Thomas A. McLaughlin
*Successful Marketing Strategies for Nonprofit Organizations* by Barry J. McLeish
*The Tax Law of Charitable Giving* by Bruce R. Hopkins
*The Tax Law of Colleges and Universities* by Bertrand M. Harding
*Tax Planning and Compliance for Tax-Exempt Organizations: Forms, Checklists, Procedures, Second Edition* by Jody Blazek
*The Universal Benefits of Volunteering: A Practical Workbook for Nonprofit Organizations, Volunteers and Corporations* by Walter P. Pidgeon, Jr.
*The Volunteer Management Handbook* by Tracy Daniel Connors

# Grantseeker's Toolkit

## A Comprehensive Guide to Finding Funding

**CHERYL CARTER NEW**
**JAMES AARON QUICK**
*of Polaris Corporation*

WILEY

**John Wiley & Sons, Inc.**
New York • Chichester • Weinheim • Brisbane • Singapore • Toronto

Published by John Wiley & Sons, Inc.
Published simultaneously in Canada.

*Library of Congress Cataloging-in-Publication Data:*

New, Cheryl Carter.
   Grantseeker's toolkit : a comprehensive guide to finding funding /
Cheryl Carter New, James Aaron Quick.
      p.    cm. — (Nonprofit law, finance, and management series)
   Includes bibliographical references and index.
   ISBN 0–471–19303–8 (pbk./disk : alk. paper)
      1. Fund raising.   2. Proposal writing for grants.   I. Quick,
James Aaron.   II. Title.   III. Series.
   HV41.2.N48   1998
   686.15′224—dc21                                         98-14681

Printed in the United States of America.

10 9 8 7 6 5 4 3

To Marlin A. Quick, the best father a boy and a man could ever have.

*—James Aaron Quick*

To Lawrence David New, my father, confidant, and soul mate. His belief in me gave me courage. I miss him.

*—Cheryl Carter New*

# Contents

# Preface

"We need money. Let's get a grant." Not only are these two phrases invariably tied together, but they usually herald the beginning of an effort so frustrating that most would-be grant writers quit (in anger or tears) before they have really begun.

It sounds so simple. "We need money. Let's get a grant." The implication is that all we have to do is tell a grant "giver" what is wanted or needed—to describe the idea—and funds will be provided. After all, anyone with a heart would give money to help with such a worthy cause. It is so obvious.

In our grants consulting business, which focuses on organizational grants, over 90 percent of the calls we receive begin, "Can you help me find a funder?" It is completely predictable—and sad. Why? Because it is starting at the wrong end of the process. It is like your team's coming to bat for the first time in the game in the bottom of the ninth. You have no plan, no team, no equipment, no managers, no track record, no hits or runs, but you want to win just the same.

The prevailing thought seems to be, "If I just knew how to find a funder, I could get a grant." Unfortunately, some do find lists of grant funders, through word-of-mouth or from a directory someone has published, before they understand the grants process. With their hearts full of hope, they write letters explaining their cause, using the same words, to all the faceless names on the lists. Then they wait expectantly for the response. The flood of "We're not awarding funds for this type of project at this time," or "We're sorry, we've already expended our funds this quarter," or more directly, "Your program doesn't meet our guidelines," turns them against grantseeking forever. We have run across people who have even become bitter and cynical, saying "They only give to their cronies," or "No one really gets these grants," or "The money's drying up anyway," or "It's rigged." The rumors spread that grantseeking is a fruitless effort in which only a favored few (with the right political pull) can succeed.

These and other misconceptions are precisely why we have spent years developing step-by-step training for potential grantseekers (and experienced ones alike). They are why we wrote this book. We want to help people start at the beginning. We want to eliminate the false expectations to end the frustration. Beyond that, we want to see good programs get the funding they deserve so that education, health care, the family, or the community can be strengthened, enhanced, and improved.

We do not have funds to grant, nor do we have the content knowledge in all these fields to directly impact improvements. We do not have the power to influence those who can make positive changes for improvement. What we do have, however, is the knowledge and skill to teach people to look at problems in education, health care, and within communities and plan for solutions. We know how to help people design projects that provide solutions to today's problems and how to teach them to describe their projects succinctly and graphically in a proposal. We know how to look at a project and at a group of funders and find the funder with an interest in solving the same problem as the project. As we share what we know with leaders in education, health care, or community development, in our own way, we help improve the quality of life for others.

Are we totally selfless? Of course not. The grants business is how we earn a living to provide dog biscuits for the office pups and to buy those noisy toys for our grandson.

More importantly, we get to be energized by being privy to some of the most exciting innovations being tested today. We get to watch the inkling of an idea spark and ignite a project that results in children, who once were "lost" to education, come alive with curiosity and the desire to learn. We get to see tested potential cures for cancer or heart disease. We get to see people in communities work together to solve their own problems with just a little help at the start, but no long-term crutches.

These activities are what grant programs are all about. They are about innovation, positive change, restructuring, renovation, and improvement—striving to make things better. Grantmakers are in the "business" of investing seed money in projects that have a good chance to do just that—to make things better. They are about helping people help themselves. They are not about giveaways or perpetual cares or soft touches. They are business people who are in the profession of promoting excellence in a field in which they have an abiding interest. Yes, some of them simply give dollars for charity (and that is related to another field called fundraising), but the preponderance of grantmakers seek plausible, attainable, testable, assessable solutions to problems they have chosen as important to solve.

Many of you have excellent ideas based on years of observation and hard work in your fields, but lack the know-how to design and develop your project, position that project so that it is marketable to a funder, or develop a proposal that describes your project effectively. We hope that in reading this book and applying the principles described herein, you succeed in acquiring the funding you need to test your solution. To help in the development of this project, this book is divided into four parts. How to Design a Fundable Project, How to Find a Funder to Match your Project, Developing the Final Project, and Developing and Writing the Final Proposal—all the steps of the grantseeking process. The computer disk included with the book offers many practical forms that you can customize as you conduct your own grantseeking process. We hope this book becomes tattered and torn while you use it as a ready reference to guide you in your efforts to improve the quality of life for others. Good luck to you in your attempts to make things better. May you earn the chance, if funds are all you need to get started, through successful grantseeking.

Cheryl Carter New
James Aaron Quick

Greenville, SC
June 1998

# Acknowledgments

For the things I know and the person that I am I credit my father; the Boy Scouts of America; high school football; the United States Marine Corps; North Carolina State University; a failed marriage and a failed business; a successful marriage and a successful business; and my teacher, my mentor, my hero, and my wife, Cheryl Carter New.

*—James Aaron Quick*

For encouragement, vision, stability, and confidence, I credit my wonderful family—each and every one of them. For love, support, guidance, values, and ambition, I credit my mother, once "just" a mother, now a best friend. For belief that it can be done, I credit all the writers in my family, especially Uncle Ted. For the will to go on, a positive outlook, and my sanity, I thank God. And certainly not least, I credit my best buddy, my rock, my true love and life's partner, my champion, James Aaron Quick.

*—Cheryl Carter New*

# How to Design a Fundable Project

# Chapter 1

# Grantseeking, The Philosophy

**E**very time a workshop is taught, there are one or two participants who are disappointed with what they hear. Why? They want a magic potion that unlocks the mystery of getting grant funding which no reputable grant consultant can give them. There is no such key. There is no shortcut.

## *The Secret*

Grantseeking is not a dance that is done with the grantmaker. It is not a mating ritual in which a certain number of head bobs and feather fluffings attract a partner; nor is it a private club where if one knows the right name and the secret handshake he or she is in the door. It is better than that. It is a negotiation in which thorough analysis, skill in problem solving, professionalism in project design, and old-fashioned effort are rewarded. We like it that way. It means that your hard work and expertise are more important than someone else's slickness and chicanery.

Does this mean the very best projects always get funded? Definitely not. After all, the process of awarding grants is mostly subjective. People review proposals and bring to the process all the baggage that people carry with them. This includes prejudices, priorities, personal viewpoints, past failures and disappointments, and all the other flotsam of life. Ask any funder over dinner and they will tell you how difficult it is to be sure you are funding an honest effort. Funders are constantly evaluating and rewriting their requests for proposal or guidelines to elicit the most pertinent information with which to judge what is, for all intents and purposes, an experiment. How a grant project is an experiment will be discussed in a later chapter, but that is exactly what most grant projects are—experiments.

The grantmaker works hard to create a review process capable of sifting through tens and hundreds and sometimes thousands of proposals and choosing the projects with the very best likelihood for success in solving the problem for which the grant money was set aside. Is the process "fair"? Well, that depends on what you call fair. If you mean does the review process distribute funds equally among the states, rural and urban sites, purple or puce programs, small and large projects, or whatever other criteria you might think up, then no, the process is not "fair." It is not supposed to be. Grantmakers choose what they wish to fund within criteria of their own design. That is the way it is. That is the way it should be. Grantmakers are investing their own funds in programs to accomplish their own missions. It does not matter much if you have the worst hard-luck case ever. What matters is if you know something that can be done to improve your situation and, moreover, if that "something" can be used elsewhere to improve a similar situation. This is the essence of what makes a project fundable.

In grantseeking, there are no hidden doors or crystal balls, no insider tricks to be uncovered. There is a straightforward process and pathway to ensuring that your proposals always wind up in the final group—the group from which the final selection is made—but it is not a secret. It is not hidden. It is right there for everyone to see. In this book, we are going to tell you about it.

To be competitive, be willing to work hard.

## It Is an Investment

Grantmaking administrators are not seeking feel-good opportunities. . . . well, maybe they are to some degree (and who could blame them), but that is not their primary purpose. Grantmaking administrators are seeking good investments. Why? There are many reasons. First, a grantmaking organization is established for the purpose of making grants. That is right, it is their job, their reason for being. They invest money for a living.

What do you think will happen to it if its administrators make bad grants? What if the administrators regularly, or even often, fund projects that are frivolous or mismanaged, or projects in which, after the grant funds are expended, there is no benefit or result, no change for the better, no new knowledge gained? That is right, they would be "fired," meaning they would not be allowed to make grants anymore. Who would fire these administrators? The directors on the boards of the grantmaking organization are responsible for hiring and firing administrators. If granted projects are weak and off the mark set by the boards of directors, then the administrators pay. This makes them very careful, sometimes, even a little suspicious.

Sometimes, however, the people who set the money aside in the first place are the administrators. What do they do if they themselves make mistakes? The answer is easy. They are more stringent in their requirements the next time they let a bid. They become tougher in analyzing the grant proposals. Just like anyone who has been bitten once, they are more careful the next time.

It is an investment. Grant funds are not given out on a whim and they are not funneled down the proverbial rat hole. To be competitive, prove that your project is a good investment, and prove that you are a good investment as well.

## It Is a Burning Desire

It has just been stated that grantmaking administrators do not make grants just to feel good. They do not, but that does not mean they have no passion. At least with regard to foundations and even corporate grantmaking organizations, most do make grants because of a burning desire to solve a problem. Yes, grantmaking organizations are tax exempt, and grant giving offers tax benefits to their sponsoring board or company. That is a fact. However, there are many other ways to gain a tax advantage than by offering grant funding.

Grantmaking organizations, both foundation and corporate, are usually established because a person or a group of people have a burning desire to solve one or more problems. Go to your local library, get a Foundation Center directory, and read the blurbs under a few listings. It does not take long to recognize the causes in which the various grantmaking foundations are interested. These causes are established by its board of directors and usually stated in the foundation bylaws or in policy statements. Projects are sought by the grantmaker that provide a solution to a problem identified by the founders or directors of the organization as being important.

There are grantmakers who specialize in solving the problems of autism, heart disease, the lack of minority young people seeking careers in the fields of science and mathematics, or the rise in school violence. Any problem that has entered the public awareness has at least one organization willing to fund projects to solve it.

Problems hurt. By definition, a problem is something that hurts or hinders someone or some activity. It can be simply a hurdle or more serious—a life-and-death barrier. When people are hurt or when they see someone hurt, they feel something. A normal person empathizes or sympathizes with the person having the problem. Perhaps the founder has experienced, or has a loved one who has experienced, the problem for which the grantmaking organization was founded. Whatever the reason, foundations usually originate from a burning desire to solve a problem.

Most federal and state government grant programs originated with heart, and some still have it. At a point in the development of the programs, some group of people had a burning desire to solve a problem. Their desire was strong enough to induce them to influence a government organization to create a grant program. Though the historical sentiment of some programs may be temporarily misplaced, the program originated from a passionate desire to solve a problem.

What is the point? The grantmaker is serious about its grants process and the results. Because of this, grantseeking is highly competitive. To attract funding, your project must have the potential of solving a problem that is very important to the grantmaker and its constituents. The grantmaker is going to be very careful about picking projects, and it will not accept a half-hearted effort. To be competitive, show the grantmaker that you believe in your project, that you are sincere in your efforts.

## It Is a Contract

A grant proposal, when accepted for funding, becomes a contract between the applicant and the grantor. What exactly is a contract? What does it mean to enter into a contract? Volumes have been written on contract law. Attorneys spend a substantial amount of their education learning about the intricacies of contracts. We venture into this subject with some trepidation, but venture we will.

A famous jurist defined a contract as "an agreement, upon sufficient consideration, to do, or not to do a particular thing." Implied in this definition are four essential components:

1. Manifestation of mutual assent
2. Consideration
3. Legality of object
4. Capacity of the parties

The "manifestation of mutual assent" is, in our case, the accepted written proposal itself. The "consideration" is twofold. On the part of the applicant, the consideration is the performance of the project as defined in the proposal. On the part of the grantor, the consideration is the providing of a certain sum of money to the applicant. The "legality of object" is simply that the whole affair and all its parts are legal. The "capacity of the parties" is that the applicant can actually perform the project as described in the proposal, and that the grantor can provide the agreed-upon funds.

This is why the person who signs the proposal must be able to enter into a contract for the applicant organization. This means that it is unlikely that the project director or the proposal writer should sign the proposal. More likely, the signer of a proposal will be someone with a position such as a school superintendent, an executive director, a president, or a chairman of the board of directors. To be competitive, take the content of the proposal seriously—it is a contract.

## It is Their Reputation

Grantmaking, as with any other vocation, has its own culture. Grantmakers know each other. They talk to each other about their successes, about projects that have accomplished striking results. Just as each of us wants to brag about good things we have done, so do administrators of grantmaking organizations. The way one is judged in this field is by projects that successfully solved a problem or provided new information that might lead someone else to solve it. In grantmaking, a job well done is the funding of a solidly designed, managed, and evaluated project. Grantmakers are constantly striving to find ways to discern good projects and submitting organizations capable of running those projects.

Grant makers attend training programs to gain the knowledge and skill to perform their responsibilities better. Many attend courses to help them develop better requests for proposals and guidelines. They meet and network and mentor, just like people do in any other profession. It is a business and a profession and a career. It is their pride and reputation that are on the line, so it is understandably important that good and great projects are chosen for funding. To be competitive, be convincing in your proposal that your project is superlative.

## It Is Your Reputation

Occasionally, we are contacted by an organization for help, when soon it becomes clear the organization really has no interest in a project. We are asked, "Can't you just come up with a project that `fits' what the funder wants and write the proposal so we can get the money?" Of course, the answer is "no." Grantseeking is not a game in which one tries to "outsmart" a grantmaker. Other than personal pride and integrity, why not? Because word gets around. Because a grant award is a contract. Because you are legally liable. Okay, so that is the extreme and it is pretty obvious that organization is either not thinking, does not understand grant seeking, or is simply unethical.

Look at another case. What about the organization that was awarded funding for a project involving the use of a computer lab. Once the computers were delivered, the organization decided the computers might have a better use administratively. When the grantmaker made a site visit, the computer lab on which the project hinged was nowhere to be seen—there was a computer here, a computer there, but no lab. Is there a difference between this organization and the first one? Maybe, maybe not.

Look at a third, more common example. Members of the organization have developed a project at a weekend retreat. The project is plausible and the development is logical. The grant is awarded. By the time the funding arrives, the administration realizes that the organization does not have the infrastructure to handle a project as complicated and intensive as the one for which the award was received. The funds are attractive, though, so the decision is made to plow on. The project sputters and is left incomplete due to mismanagement and inattention.

Three different examples, three different sets of intentions, all with the same result. The organization that takes the money and runs; the organization that takes the money and does not fulfill the contract; and the organization that gets in over its head have all three probably made themselves ineligible for further funding. Word gets out. A track record of deception, negligence, or incompetence is as hard to live down in the grants world as it is anywhere else. The hardest grant to get is the first. After that, it is up to you. To be competitive, establish a track record of integrity, sincerity, and competence.

## It Is Our Future

Fortunately, money is not the answer to all the world is problems. However, because money buys resources—employees, books, consulting expertise, paper, stamps, telephone time, copiers, computers, vans, and swimming pools—it undergirds the activities necessary for most solutions.

There are many creative, dedicated people with great ideas who do not have sufficient funds to implement them; additional money is needed for a successful project launching. Organizations with the burning desire for solutions may have money, but certainly not enough to take on the whole problem, to "cure world hunger," all in one fell swoop. No one has that kind of money, not even Bill Gates.

What is the solution? Grant programs. Grantmaking is a key to continuing rational experimentation, practical innovation, positive change, and healthy speculation. Grant makers provide the seed money necessary to encourage those people with few or no resources, but with exceptional analysis, planning, organizing and implementation skills, to try new things or update and revise old ones.

Think of all the activities grant funding supports: education programs for handicapped children, for emotionally disturbed and mentally challenged individuals, and for children disadvantaged by nature of their economic condition; medical research to cure heart disease, cancer, acquired immune deficiency syndrome (AIDS), and clinical depression; community health programs to stop fetal alcohol syndrome, tuberculosis, and drug abuse; community development programs to provide low-income housing, recreation centers for teens, adult literacy opportunities, and fitness centers for the elderly. These are just a few examples; they only scratch the surface. Grantmakers contribute immeasurably to the improvement of the quality of life in the world community. Yes, the world community. Grant funds reach all corners of the world, and not just from U.S. organizations, but from grantmaking sources all over from Australia to Czechoslovakia, from Honduras to Siberia.

As the world moves faster and faster, problems change—and with the increasing pace of life, even proliferate—more and more money will be allocated to grant efforts. It is only logical. How else can innovation be effectively financed? Money for grants has increased every year even through tough economic times. There may have been slowdowns in the speed of growth, but there has been growth all the same. Some programs may be eliminated because they do not work, are outdated, or become unpopular, but others begin.

Grantmaking is big business and it is serious business. It has to do with our future.

To be competitive, follow, to the letter, the process taught in this book.

## Organization of This Book

The overall purpose of this book, as with all our grantseeking work with clients, is to get your grant proposal into the top 10 percent. That is where the competition takes place. When you consistently place your proposals in the top 10 percent, you will get 3 to 4 out of every 10 submitted proposals funded. This will make you a grants superstar.

The basic concept of this book is of a set of step-by-step forms with explanations on how to complete them. The forms are found on the computer disk in the back cover. The explanations are in the book. The grant-seeking process is divided into five major parts.

1. How to Design a Fundable Project
2. How to Find a Matching Funding Source
3. How to Analyze Funder Guidelines or Request for Proposal (RFP)
4. How to Develop the Project, In-depth
5. How to Write the Proposal

These five steps constitute the entire grant-seeking process. Everything starts with a project that is a solution to a problem. Designing this project is the first major step in successful grant seeking. Without a project, none of the other steps can be completed.

Once a project exists, a source to which to apply for funding must be found. This is the outcome of the four step-by-step processes to find a federal, foundation, corporate, or state or local funding source. Once a funding source is found, the application guidelines or the request for proposal (RFP) must be analyzed. This analysis will guide one in two ways. The first is in modifying our project so it fits with the grantor's agenda. The other is to give us directions for creating the proposals.

Now, the project can be fully developed. At its most basic, full project development consists of answering several questions about every aspect of the project plan, such as: What will happen? Who will do it? When will it happen? What resources will be needed to do it? How much money will it cost to do it?

Only after all four steps are finished is one ready to write a proposal. Proposal writing is not the main job of a grantseeker. More than three quarters of a grantseeker's time should be spent designing solutions to problems, finding funding sources, analyzing RFPs, and fully developing projects. The actual writing of the proposal becomes relatively easy once you know what goes into the proposal, and you know what you are going to write about—your project.

This, then, is the organization of this book. You will find four parts, covering the steps listed. Associated with each part are forms found on the computer disk included with the book. Follow the step-by-step directions. Fill out all the forms. When you finish, you will have a grant proposal that will land in the top 10 percent. This gives you a 30 to 40 percent chance of winning each and every time you apply.

# Chapter 2

# Where To Begin?

## *Come Back to the Problem*

"Where do I begin?"

The answer is simple. It does not matter where, but always come back to the problem.

Most often people actually begin at the end of the process, with "things" they want and "things" they need. This, again, is evidenced by the questions raised by grantseekers.

- "Where can I find a list of funders that fund technology?"
- "We need a new widget, who can you recommend?"
- "Is there anyone who would pay for a swimming pool?"
- "Our kids do not have a blodgett."
- "We have a good program idea, but can't fund the software."
- "I have this whole file of items we need—we asked each department to make a list."

All "things" . . . everyone has his or her own list of things without which something really bad will happen. But what? What will happen if these things are not acquired? This is the first question grantseekers need to ask themselves when looking over their list.

Why are particular things on the list in the first place? Because there was a problem. If not, then there is no reason to need them. Problems provide a purpose for the things on our needs list. Look at the list above and track back to the problems that caused the "thing" to be put on the needs list in the first place.

- "Where can I find a list of funders that fund technology?"

What is behind this question? Grantseekers often picture computers, record players, television screens, modems, testing equipment, test tubes, and even satellite dishes and such. But why? Why do you need computers? If the answer is, "Well, everyone knows every classroom should have at least 10 computers," the organization needs to think this through again. No investor will accept the argument that "we need" these because everyone else has them. As a parent, would you accept this from your child? What happens when your teenager comes to you and says, "I need a cell phone because every other guy in school has one." Why do you need it, son? "Oh, just because every other guy has one and I want to be cool." Is this a good enough reason? Certainly not.

So return to the drawing board. Why does the school need computers? According to your observations, test scores and feedback from teachers, parents, and local employers, there is a serious problem. The reading and writing skills of children in your school district are severely lacking. One local project developed in conjunction with the local employers as well as parents is a mentoring project in which regular correspondence will take place between children in your schools, their parents in various business locations throughout your city, and by virtue of the local companies, with people in all walks of life in subsidiary locations throughout the country. It is a very good bet that children will be motivated to work hard on their communication skills to participate in the program. One of the things needed is computers.

From "we need computers" to a multipartner, multistate mentoring and motivation model for teaching written communication skills is a very large leap. It is a large leap from not fundable to highly fundable. The following is another example.

- "Is there anyone who would pay for a swimming pool?"

If the above question was answered as it appears on the surface, without asking any questions, the answer would be, "No, not a grant funder anyway." Look at this further. For what purpose are you going to use the swimming pool?

What a good idea! The community has a large elderly population and they are dying way too young. It is a rural Southern community with traditional habits that include yummy, but deadly, combinations of high-fat and fried cooking. In a community meeting, it was found that they would love a swimming pool all their own. There is one for the youth of the community, but the seniors are not too happy with the noise and commotion and family pools are still populated with small children and lots of splashing. "Why isn't there a Y-Senior?" one lady asked.

There are enough elderly citizens to keep a pool full all day and most of the evening. The local health care and community service groups have the idea to develop a senior recreation center with activities, classes, volunteer opportunities, and a staffed on-line information area for answering the myriad of questions about insurance, health care, Social Security, and so on. It will be a seniors-only country club, available to all citizens of a certain age from all walks of life. Various groups have patched together or raised funds for most of the other services, and a local builder has promised the building, but you still need the pool.

This project could be a model for other communities as our population becomes grayer and the baby boomers crash through the time barrier into old age. When placed in the larger social framework, this project becomes very fundable in the eyes of the grantmaker.

## Grantseeking or Fundraising?

Grantseeking begins with a problem. If the onion of grantseeking is peeled through all its layers, at the very core you find a problem. Grantmakers, be they government organizations, foundations, or corporations, make grants to fund solutions to problems. If you have an item that you simply want, for your organization, but that item is not really connected to any kind of problem, then fundraising is the best avenue to obtain the funds.

How does fundraising differ from grantseeking? Fundraising, generally speaking, is a companion effort to a grant effort and should be used to support grant projects. The converse is also true. Fundraising does not normally depend on presentation of a proposal. It does not necessarily require a needs analysis and problem statement, although problem definition is certainly involved in many cases. It takes great skill to be a good fundraiser, but it is a different kind of effort.

In fundraising, the organization says, "We want a community center," or "We want to establish an endowment for our college. Please donate funds to be placed in trust to establish our endowment," or "Please contribute to our annual fundraising campaign. The money goes for a good cause, to support your local heart association." The request is usually in the form of a letter, a phone call, or a personal meeting. Fundraising is a more direct request for funds. Fundraisers rely on events to raise awareness of an issue. Fundraisers work with past contributors, alumni associations, and benefactors. Fundraisers look for donors who will bequeath funds in their wills.

Grantseekers, on the other hand, are really responding to a published interest in receiving competitive proposals by grantmakers. Grantmakers may publicize their efforts strongly and visibly or simply have a blurb in a directory somewhere.

Each grant proposal is unique to the particular funder one is approaching. Whereas in fundraising, one letter may be sent to many potential contributors; this approach guarantees failure in grantseeking.

## The Connection

Grantseekers are really linked to grantmakers by virtue of an interest in solving the same problem. What grantseekers do to solve the problem is termed a project or program. The way the grantseeker communicates with the grantmaker is through a proposal that usually just answers questions about the project posed by the grantmaker. That is the connection.

Those who seek grants need to study the situation and concentrate on solving the problems. Develop projects to do so. Then, and only then, go looking for funders. They will be found by virtue of their interest in the same problem you intend to solve.

## Using the Connection to Do It Right

Most grantmakers have deadlines for submission of proposals. Rather than reviewing proposals year round, there is a certain time (or several times) a year when the grantmaker reviews all proposals submitted for that particular offering. Often, the time from when you find out that a grantmaker is letting a request to the deadline can be very brief. Many a grantseeker gets a notice from his or her employer on December 17 with a January 1 deadline. However, the difference in whether this is just a troublesome occurrence or a family crisis is in whether the organization is doing it right. If, when presented with the December request, there is a rush of holiday shopping and giving up that holiday house tour, then that is one thing. It is a problem, but not a crisis. If, however, it means facing no trimming, farming out dear old Aunt Ida to other relatives, and ordering take-out Chinese for the holiday dinner, then that is quite another. However, if it is done right, the writing of the proposal should not take very long.

That last statement bears repeating. If it is done right, the writing of the proposal should not take very long. Writing the proposal should be about 10 to 15 percent of the issue.

Why is this so often not the case? The reason is that people too frequently pick up the funder's guidelines or RFP and start writing. Never mind that they really do not have anything concrete about which to write. Grantmakers do not want a stream of consciousness flow of prose about your good, but half-baked, idea. They want answers to the questions about the good and very well-developed project!

What do you do? Work within the organization to consistently plan for solving problems. Design projects, not in full detail, but at least on paper, with good chances for solving the problems faced every day. Keep these in a file or in notebooks on a shelf for when a grant program that matches arises.

Never start writing a grant proposal without first designing and developing a solid project about which to write. How is that done? This book will act as a guide through all the steps of project design, project development, funder research, and proposal writing. Read through the book from cover to cover first. Mark pages, underline phrases, and highlight sections to help you find the sections you need to review when you start your next grantseeking project. Use the book as a reference and follow the process, and you will consistently put your proposals in the top 10 percent of those received by the funder. That is the best you can do. You can not account for the subjective decisions of the reviewers, but you can be competitive each and every time you submit.

An often asked question is, "What percentage of grant proposals get funded?" The answer is a high of 20 to 25 percent for some state programs to less than one percent at many foundations. What percentage of proposals submitted by a master grantseeker get funded? The answer to that question is 30 to 40 percent.

Therefore, grantseeking is, across the board, a job at which the organization will fail more often than it succeeds. That is the way it is. How exactly does one succeed at a job when one fails more often than one succeeds?

Consider baseball. One can no doubt agree that one of the jobs of a major league baseball player is to go to the plate and get base hits. What, then, happens to a major league baseball player when he fails to do his job 7 times out of 10—70 percent of the time. Just what happens to this miserable failure?

He is called a superstar and is paid millions of dollars a year. If he does it over his entire career, the chances are strong that he will be in the Baseball Hall of Fame. He will be a legend of the game by failing to get a hit 70 percent of the time.

If a grantseeker succeeds 30 to 40 percent of the time with your grant proposals, they will be a grants superstar and will bring hundreds of thousands of dollars into their organization. If there is a secret to grantseeking, it is to follow the grantor's directions and keep submitting proposals. If the win ratio is 3 out of 10, then it can be determined exactly how many proposals to submit to receive the funds that are needed. It is really that simple. Keep doing it, and keep doing it. If three winners are needed this year, submit 10 proposals. If six winners are needed this year, submit 20 proposals. If nine winners are needed this year, submit 30 proposals. Do the math. Submit the proposals.

## Defining the Real Problem

Grantseeking begins with a problem. It is the reason grant funds are being sought—to solve a problem. As previously stated, it is the match, the connection between the organization, as the grantseeker, and the grantmaker. Grantmakers award grants to solve problems. At the core of every grant proposal, at its heart, lies a problem statement.

What are these problems? How can a problem be defined? The dictionary says that a problem is "a question proposed for a solution." That is a start, but what exactly is a question? The same dictionary says that a question is "a problem." Hmmm—it seems we are being led in a tight little circle. Look further. Another word often used in grantseeking as a synonym for "problem" is "need." Our friend Webster says that a need is "a lack of something useful or required." A lack of something useful is an easy idea to grasp. Teen pregnancy, poverty, illiteracy, cancer, domestic violence, child abuse, unemployment—all of these clearly bespeak a lack of something useful, something required. In general, in grantseeking, a problem means a lack of something useful, be it education, motivation, food, a job, self-esteem, health, or any other such thing.

So, what is *your organization's* problem? A teacher's answer is likely to be "low test scores." A health care professional: "People are dying too young." A law enforcement officer: "We are beginning to have youth problems—vandalism is on the rise." A community planner: "Our city accident statistics show over 90 percent occurring to folks over 60." A parent: "My child is one of a big group who is in the fourth grade and still can not read." These are tough topics all right, but they're not problems.

"Not problems?! You go tell our parents and the school board that low test scores aren't a problem! We've got our administrators, politicians, the press, and parents all over us about low test scores. Don't tell me it's not a problem!"

Low test scores certainly do cause problems. However they are really symptoms, not the problem. The real issues—the causes—of the low test scores, the causes of rising juvenile violence, the causes of high accident rates in the elderly population, and the causes of fourth graders not being able to read are something else altogether.

Back to low test scores. It takes only a few minutes with a group of educators and parents for the real causes of low test scores to emerge:

lack of motivation, absenteeism, lack of parental support, poor tests, poor teachers, poor facilities, and so on. There is absolutely nothing to be done directly about low test scores. It is too broad a topic. Think of a fourth grader who has just been assigned his or her first grade school paper. With enthusiasm, the topic proudly presented to the teacher is *Animals Throughout History*. The teacher gently explains that it might have been better if one animal and one point in time had been chosen. It is the same with problem solving and with grantseeking. The more narrowed down and focused the sites are on a target, the better the project design. Low test scores will be improved by combating the cause—the real problem.

Grantmakers require that you present them with a project that solves a problem about which you have a mutual interest. The symptom is what gets the big press, the public attention. Symptoms are headline grabbers. However, the real problem, the underlying cause, is where solutions take place. As a rule of thumb, when someone asks, "What's the problem," the first answer is likely to be a symptom, not the real problem. We call these symptoms "Broad Problems" because they are very broad and general. Broad Problems are not a bad place to start project development, but they are a terrible place to end it. Following is a step-by-step process to follow, along with explanations and examples, to help you get beneath the Broad Problems to the causes, or Real Problems, which form the foundation of every fundable project.

## WHAT IS YOUR REAL PROBLEM?—AN EXERICISE  0201.DOC

### Step One: List Broad Problems  0201.DOC

Stating a problem should not be very hard. After all, they slap us in the face every day. The first exercise to do, then, is to sit quietly and write them down. Make a list, as has been done in Exhibit 2.1. A blank version of the form and all the other exercise forms (where a disk icon appears) can be found on the disk.

Do any of these look familiar? They should. They are right out of your regional newspapers. Can you tackle them all? No, of course not. The problem an organization takes on is determined by the purpose and scope of your organization. There are many ways to narrow down the topic and one way is for each organization (or, better yet, group of partnering organizations) to take on one or two problems as its mission. Focus on the one that makes the most sense to you and your organization.

In hundreds of workshops across the country, the single biggest stumbling block when developing an initial problem statement is that

## Exhibit 2.1

### Broad Problems List

- We have a high rate of teen pregnancy in our community.
- There are too many students not finishing high school.
- Drug abuse is growing.
- The incidents of reported child abuse are increasing.
- Youth vandalism has skyrocketed.
- Domestic violence is on the rise.
- Local employers are reporting that our graduates have low reading and writing skills.
- More homeless people are gathering down at the central park.
- We actually had a few elderly people die of heat stroke (or cold, depending on where you live), shut up in their houses.
- The emergency room at the hospital is overwhelmed by all the indigent cases on the weekends.

---

people begin immediately to discuss the gear, the paraphernalia, of a solution.

- "We need more room."
- "We need another resident facility."
- "We've just got to get space for 10 to 15 more people."
- "We need a swimming pool."
- "Band instruments . . . we need band instruments."

All are the paraphernalia of a solution. Picture a solution as a critter—a little munchkin with a backpack. Hanging out of the backpack are all these things, all dangling down. These things will be needed somewhere along the line to help the solution along, but they are not, in and of themselves, the solution itself. They are just "things." They are tools to be used.

If the organization looks at the list and sees a group of tools, put the tools aside for later. The problem is not that you need more room, another resident facility, space for more people, a swimming pool, or band instruments. These are tools you'll need to solve the problem, but their lack is not the problem itself.

Here is an example. Some people have difficulty getting to libraries to acquire reading and other learning materials. They have no reliable transportation or they live too far away and the library is too difficult for them to access. The solution? Take the library to them. Develop a project that succeeds in bringing the library to the folks that need it but can not get to it. To do this, several things are required. One necessity might be a van with shelving and other storage to hold library materials. A driver and other staff will be needed for the van, along with a good system for checking out, tracking, and retrieving materials. Then there is a project component devoted to spreading the word about the availability of this service and scheduling is another component. It does not take long to see how large and complex a project this will become before it is completely planned and implemented. If an organization did not know better and you was asked, "What's your problem?" it might have answered, "We need a van." You see, the van is just a tool. It certainly isn't the problem, nor is it the project. It is just a tool.

Look at another solution to this same problem with another project. The problem, remember, is that folks can not access the materials in the library because they have no reliable transportation or they live too far away and the library is too difficult for them to access. The first solution was a mobile library. However, what if we make most of the library services available using on-line communications as well as the mail and other delivery services. Our project allows people to check out materials by electronic mail and have them delivered to their doors with a return shipping slip for sending the materials back to the library. In addition, a toll-free data access capability is added for searching library databases and reading newspapers and other such electronically friendly services. Now, some of the isolated people can access the library and its materials right from their own homes. The same problem was solved, but with another project. Does one project, the mobile van, preclude the need for the other project, electronic access? No, some people will use one service and some the other.

What's your problem? If asked, would you say, "We need phone lines?" Not now, you wouldn't. You would know better!

### Step Two: Choose a Broad Problem and List the Causes  0201.DOC

Look back at your list of Broad Problems. Pick one problem on which to concentrate. Write it down in the space provided on the worksheet. List the things you think are the likely causes of the Broad Problem. One way to get at likely causes is to ask yourself, "Why?" In the case of the example in Exhibit 2.2, the question to answer might be, "Why has youth vandalism skyrocketed in our community?" Under "Likely Causes," all the answers to the question are listed.

This exercise should provide broad causes to the broad problem—think of everything possible.

## EXHIBIT 2.2

### Broad Problems and List of Causes

Broad Problem—Youth vandalism has skyrocketed in our community.

**Likely Causes**

- Too little parental supervision
- Too little community supervision
- Nothing for young people to do
- Lots of kids 13–19
- Few school or church activities
- Not many street lights or night security lights
- Many vacation homes that are empty most of time
- Not enough police officers
- No organized "watch" groups
- Some stores lax about carding young people
- Buildings very close together with lots of alleys

*Step Three: Cross Out*  0201.DOC

Look at the list. There are usually several items that, though true enough, can not be changed—at least not by the organization or not at this time. Cross through the things the organization can not do anything about, as there is no point in worrying about things that can not be corrected. Look at Exhibit 2.2. The fact that there are lots of teens certainly increases the likelihood of youth vandalism since there is safety in numbers, but there is not much you can do about the numbers. So cross that one off the list. You probably can not increase the number of officers on the police force or the way the buildings are built, so those go off too. You can not, and would not want to, keep people from having vacation homes. Draw lines through all those.

*Step Four: Circle*  0201.DOC

Now look at your list. Circle any of the causes with which your organization has a direct relationship, as we did in Exhibit 2.3. If the organization is a youth service organization, a school, a church, or a community development group, then several items on the list will be circled.

**Exhibit 2.3**

## Circling Direct Relationships

Broad Problem—Youth vandalism has skyrocketed in our community.

### Likely Causes

- Too little parental supervision
- Too little community supervision
- Nothing for young people to do
- ~~Lots of kids 13–19~~
- Few school or church activities
- Not many street lights or night security lights
- ~~Many vacation homes that are empty most of time~~
- ~~Not enough police officers~~
- No organized "watch" groups
- Some stores lax about carding young people
- ~~Buildings very close together with lots of alleys~~

*Step Five: Group*  0201.DOC

Study the causes circled in your exercise. Are they closely connected or somewhat separate? Group the things that are very closely related, as seen in Exhibit 2.4. In our example, the groupings might look like this.

In Exhibit 2.4, parent and community supervision are closely related causes, since they are both connected to observation of and attention to community young people. Activities for youth can be developed around both schools and churches, thus providing something for young people to do, so these items are associated. The odd item is the laxness of some businesses in carding people before selling alcoholic beverages and other regulated products.

*Step Six: Choose*  0201.DOC

Our example organization may, in fact, decide to work on all three groupings of causes listed. However, each grouping deserves a separate project. The more well-defined the problem, the more likely the project will be fundable. Therefore, it is important to choose a reasonably narrowly defined problem.

EXHIBIT 2.4

## Grouping Related Causes

Broad Problem—Youth vandalism has skyrocketed in our community.

**Likely Causes**

- Too little parental supervision
- Too little community supervision
- Nothing for young people to do
- Few school or church activities
- Some stores lax about carding young people

---

From the grouped list in Exhibit 2.4, choose the grouped causes: too little parental supervision and too little community supervision. Focus the project on these two related causes.

### Step Seven: Specify the Target Population       0201.DOC

Go back to an earlier point, the confusing idea of "things," the tools that are needed with the problem. One reason many organizations have a hard time letting go of the things they need so they can work directly on the real problem is that they have lost, forgotten, or misplaced their target population. It is *not* "What do I as an administrator need?" It is *not* "What do we as employees need?" It is not even "What do we as an organization need?" That's right. It *is* "What is needed to serve the target population?" It is "How can the organization do a better job for those they are serving?" In grantseeking, those the organization serves, however it serves them, are always first. Everything comes from and points to them. The organization is asking for assistance only as a means to achieve this end.

For example, an organization may want to say, "Our problem is that our staff lacks training." The way it arrived at this conclusion was by noting that staff are not providing the services or products they should and could because they do not know how. The focus is really on providing better services and products for the target population; one way to do that is to train the staff to be more effective. However, what the organization said does not reflect its thinking. It said, "We need training." "We" refers to the organization and its staff. In grant terms, "We need training" in and of itself is not fundable. In grant terms, "We're going to provide our staff with the knowledge and skills they need to adapt the physical therapy activities to accommodate children with cerebral palsy," is definitely the core of a fundable project. Note the difference. Here is another example.

"We need computers." If an organization goes to a grantmaker with that request, it will get turned down. Why? Because that statement can be responded to with, "So what." Never allow a grantmaker to think "so what" about your request.

If the request can be answered with "so what," then think through why it is made. How does it relate to the target population? "We need computers." Why? For what will they be used? Suppose it is for a class of gifted students who should be taught high-level research skills using all types of research avenues, both primary and secondary. To teach them to use all the current tools available, computers are needed. This makes sense to a grantmaker. The focus is clearly on the target population.

If an organization is typical, it serves many target populations and many combinations of populations. If you are an educator, your target populations are: the student body; the at-risk students in the fourth grade; first graders who do not have all their immunizations; gifted seniors; preschoolers from single-parent families; migrant children; children who can not read at grade level; boys; girls; Hispanic middle-school students; Native American preschoolers . . . the list could literally go on forever.

What if you are a physical therapist? Your target populations may be: people with hand injuries; children with cerebral palsy; obese people with knee problems; construction and heavy industry workers with low back pain; women; men; children; pregnant ladies; old folks; babies; people recovering from broken bones . . . again, the list could go on and on. You also serve many target populations.

Make a list of as many of the target populations and combinations of populations that serve as you can think of. Think of all the combinations due to a special characteristic such as ability, health problem, gift and skill, or challenge. Think of all combinations due to age, sex, or condition.

After you have made your large list, then look back at Step Six: Choose one grouping on which to concentrate for your project. Now, identify the target population for which you will design your project. Be as specific as possible.

Return to the example Broad Problem in Exhibit 2.5. Remember that our Broad Problem was "Youth vandalism has skyrocketed in our community." Several causes were listed, and the ones our organization would logically tackle were put into three groupings. Any of the three groupings could be grounds for a grants project.

For purposes of illustration, we will choose one of the groupings with two parts: (1) too little parental supervision, and (2) too little commu-

EXHIBIT 2.5

## Determining the Target Population

*Broad Problem*—Youth vandalism has skyrocketed in our community.

*Cause (Real Problem)*—(1) too little parental supervision, and (2) too little community supervision.

*Target Population*—middle school children, average ages 12 to 14.

nity supervision. You may choose a single stand-alone cause. We could have chosen the stand-alone cause: Some stores are lax about carding young people.

After you have chosen your grouping or single issue, then write down the target population for that issue. You may have several target populations listed when you are finished, or the cause may be linked clearly to just one.

In this case, we will target middle school children, average ages 12 to 14.

## *Conclusion*

You have now completed the first steps in getting a grant. Here is one more review of the seven steps we have done so far before we go on.

1. List Broad Problems—we listed the Broad Problems.
2. Choose one and list causes—we chose one of our Broad Problems and listed the causes of it.
3. Cross Out—we eliminated those causes we could not do anything about.
4. Circle—we circled the causes with which our organization has a direct relationship.
5. Group—we grouped related circled causes.
6. Select—we selected one grouping of causes on which to concentrate for our project. We also call these causes the Real Problem.
7. Specify—we specified a target population for the cause or real problem we selected in Step Six.

# Chapter 3

# Designing the Project

## *Begin with the Problem*

Now that the Broad Problem has been defined (written down), and now that it is clear that this Broad Problem is a symptom of the Real Problem, which is in reality a cause of the symptom, it is time to create the solution. This solution is the project. In grantseeking, remember, projects are solutions to problems.

How does this work? Does the project appear from thin air? No. However, a grantseeker has the knowledge and expertise, as a professional in his or her field, to design a fundable project. It is in there. Refer again to the example from Chapter 2.

As can be seen in Exhibit 3.1, the community is having a serious vandalism problem. This is the Broad Problem. From police reports, eyewitnesses, rumor, and hard evidence, it can be determined that the perpetrators are juveniles. There are many potential causes for this problem, but some of them are beyond our scope and abilities. The causes have been narrowed down, and two closely related causes have been chosen to work on. These are the Real Problems that will be worked on with the project. It is determined that there is not enough parental supervision and community supervision in our community. Children are left alone, unattended, for many hours during the day. There are blocks of time during which teens roam around the community in groups with little to occupy their time and no adult oversight.

The worst cases of vandalism occur in the 15-to-18 age group, so it is decided to first target children slightly younger to try to stop the problem before it starts. A secondary project may be designed that directly impacts the 15-to-18 age group, but one thing at a time. The more narrow the scope of the project, the more chance for success and the easier it will be to evaluate progress.

EXHIBIT 3.1

## Defining the Problem

*Broad Problem*—Youth vandalism has skyrocketed in our community.

*Cause (Real Problem)*—(1) too little parental supervision, and (2) too little community supervision

*Target Population*—middle school children, average ages 12 to 14

Logically, what could be done, in a project to combat the identified problem? Consider the Real Problem(s) targeted in Chapter 2. Then, ask yourself several questions.

*Real Problems*

(1) too little parental supervision, and (2) too little community supervision

- How could this be countered, reversed, or turned around?
- How can we gain more parental supervision?
- How can we affect more community supervision?

The hypothetical project is to initiate a buddy-system teen supervision program involving parents, area businesses and industries, community agencies, and religious leaders. A board of directors will be formed, with representatives from each group to oversee efforts. A project director and support staff will be hired on the project budget, who will answer to the board. Questionnaires, focus groups, and town meetings will be used to identify activities and topics to include in a community-wide teen support program. Mini-courses will be offered in locations throughout the community, easily accessible to all, concerning counseling and coping topics that lend themselves to the group workshop setting. For those parents who work and cannot be at home when their children come home from school, their children will have available at least two community options where the children can go after school until the parents return home. These options may include sports programs, employer-sponsored learning opportunities, after-school programs, and others identified by committees working with the board and the project director. There are many more potential components for this project, but these are enough for an illustration.

Look back at the Real Problems we identified: (1) too little parental supervision, and (2) too little community supervision. Then, reread the beginning project description. Can you see how our project answers the question "How?" about the problem on which we have chosen to work? Ask yourself the question "How?" about your broad problem.

## *Evidence of the Problem*

Before continuing with project design, it is important re-evaluate the evidence of our problem. Ensure that it is not just the organization's opinion but that there is real evidence that the problem exists. Writing a grant proposal has some similarities to writing a research or term paper or thesis. Proof of the existence is critical because the problem is what the whole project is based on.

Does one have to prove everything? For example, in Exhibit 3.2, is there a lack of evidence that there is a teen pregnancy problem in America? No, teen pregnancy is a Broad Problem, and Broad Problems are those that are foremost in the public consciousness. Professional journals and popular news magazines alike contain articles about the problem. Local newspapers devote space to discussions of the problem. The problem is accepted, it is legitimate. If the Broad Problem targeted by an organization has not made it into the public consciousness, it may not be a good one on which to found a project at this time. It may be too narrowly recognized to have yet attracted grantmakers. However, usually, unless specifically asked by the grantmaker for proof of the Broad Problem, an organization does not really have to prove it. What does have to be

### EXHIBIT 3.2

### Step Eight: List Evidence of the Problem

Write your Broad Problem and Real Problem(s) in the space indicated. To the right, list evidence (birth records, test scores, surveys, etc.) that the problem exists. For each bit of evidence, indicate where it can be found.

| Broad Problem<br>Real Problem(s) | Evidence | Location of<br>Evidence |
| --- | --- | --- |
| Teen Pregnancy | Birth Records | Hospitals |
| Real Problem: | Counselor's Observations | Schools/Social Services |
| Lack of understanding | Surveys | Schools/Social Services |
|   on part of teens of | Questionnaire's of Teens | Schools/Social Services |
|   what is involved in | Health Statistics | Health Department |
|   raising a child. | Abortion Statistics | Health Department |

proven, however, is that the Broad Problem exists in the community—the one in which the program will be implemented. Therefore, it is not necessary to prove that teen pregnancy is a problem nationally, but that statistics show it is a problem in your community.

Look at another example. Suppose the Broad Problem is increasing spousal abuse. The media, from *Ladies Home Journal* to CNN, report that incidents of spousal abuse are on the rise. An organization intends to base its project on this Broad Problem. The cause, or Real Problem, the organization has chosen is the "victim" attitude of both women and men that may set them up for abuse. To have a legitimate project, an organization must have a valid problem. If there are no incidents of spousal abuse in its community, how is the organization going to do a project? What is it going to compare to measure your results? Obviously, the organization needs to compare incidents of abuse before and after your project to see if your project has done any good. The grantmaker is going to want to know that a local problem with spousal abuse exists. What evidence is available? Where would an organization get that evidence?

### Step Eight: List Evidence of the Problem  0301.DOC

Again, look at the worksheet in Exhibit 3.2. Note that there are spaces on the left for you to list the Broad Problem and also the causes, or Real Problems, you have chosen to undertake with your project. List them one after the other in the spaces provided. You may be targeting only one cause or Real Problem, rather than a group of them, so it is okay just to list one Real Problem.

To the right of the Broad Problem and the Real Problem you have listed, list the evidence of that problem that probably exists. Look at one of the examples. The first project discussed was to be based on the Broad Problem of teen pregnancy. Suppose the real problem is the lack of understanding of teens of the responsibilities of raising a child. Teen Pregnancy has been written in the space for the Broad Problem on the worksheet, and the Real Problem has been listed. What evidence do you have that teen pregnancy is a problem for your community? Here are some pieces of evidence that come to mind: birth records, counselor's observations, surveys and questionnaires of teens, health statistics, and abortion statistics, to name a few.

The last column is where you will record the locations of the evidence you have listed. In the example, birth records will be found through hospitals and clinics; counselors are in the schools, and social service agencies and surveys and questionnaires are likely to be found there as well;

health statistics and abortion statistics will be found at the health department at the local, county, and state levels.

You are just in the process of project design right now, but later on you will need this worksheet to guide someone in acquiring the information you need to prove the problem exists in your community. This worksheet is available on the disk.

### *Step Nine: Brainstorm Project Ideas*  0302.DOC

The next step is to answer the "how" question. In direct relation to the Real Problem(s) you have chosen to tackle, and given your professional experience, education, training, and skill, brainstorm a project solution. Brainstorming requires extreme flexibility and lack of rigidity regarding the ideas presented by members of the group. The leader should keep the discussion focused on the Real Problems on which the group has chosen to work; otherwise, people should be able to be creative. Exhibit 3.3 contains the Brainstorming Rules of Engagement, and can be used in conjunction with the form found on the disk.

In addition to the Rules of Engagement, Exhibit 3.4 is a Question Guide, a tool, to help you lead a group of people in brainstorming.

At the end of this exercise, you should have several good suggestions about how to solve this problem—the solution may be among them.

### Exhibit 3.3

## Brainstorming Rules of Engagement

1. A time frame is set for the session. You need at least one hour.
2. The Broad Problem, Real Problem, and Target Population are presented by a leader.
3. One person must be a recorder.
4. After the leader presents the problem, solution ideas (project ideas) are suggested by members of the brainstorming group.
5. Ideas will be stated in this form: "My project idea is XX." Those presenting ideas must simply state them.
6. The recorder simply listens to an idea and writes the idea down with no editing. Initial each idea.
7. Members of the group may ask for clarification if they do not understand the idea.
8. No ideas are discussed by the group. There is no debate.
9. The leader (or leadership committee) uses the brainstormed ideas to help in the development of a project that solves a problem.

## Exhibit 3.4

### Brainstorming Question Guide

To effectively lead a brainstorming session, good questioning techniques are needed. Following is information about various questioning techniques that can be used to facilitate your brainstorming session.

#### Indirect Questions

Indirect questions are used to get complete descriptions of project ideas from participants. Indirect questions

- Cannot be answered "yes" or "no"
- Begin with why, how, what
- Other than focusing on the Real Problem, don't guide participants in any particular direction
- Elicit elaboration of ideas
- Promote individual discovery of ideas

Examples of indirect questions include:

- How do you think we could solve this problem?
- If money were no object, what would you do to solve the problem?
- If you were in charge, how would you solve this problem?
- How do you think we could set up that part of the project?
- What type of partner would we need?

#### Direct Questions

Direct questions require a "yes," "no," or brief answer. Direct questions are used to specify key points in discussion. They are not intended to create further discussion, rather to make decisions. Direct questions

- Nail down specific facts
- Usually begin with where, when, who, how many, how much
- Are useful to keep the group on task
- Are useful to clarify ideas
- Can be used to elicit participation

Examples of direct questions include:

- How much time do you think it will take?
- How could it be done better another way?
- Who should take the lead in the project?
- When is the best time to begin?
- Where would we house this project?

# *Project Considerations*

At this point in the process, it is time to make some concrete decisions about the project. Though this book will provide some guidance, you are mostly on your own. Projects take many shapes and come in many sizes. The steps are the same, but the work you do will be very different depending on whether your project is about research, education, health care, testing and evaluation, community action, or social service.

### *Step Ten: Make Project Choices*

The next step is to study all the project ideas and decide the makeup of one that will be most effective in providing a solution to the identified problem. The organization should have the seeds of many good projects by this time in the process. In fact, it should have many projects in various stages of development at all times, regardless of whether the organization is applying for grant funding. It is when we lose sight of this fact that we cease to improve our work, our organization, and more importantly our services or products for the people we serve. To continue the process of developing a fundable project, an organization needs to concentrate on just one. Once it has completed that one, then it can go back through the process with another and another so, eventually, it will have many projects on the grants "hit list."

> You should have many projects in various stages of development at all times, regardless whether you apply for grant funding. It is when we lose sight of this fact that we cease to improve our work, our organization, and more importantly our services or products for the people we serve.

The chosen project must be solidly founded in the appropriate principles for the subject matter. If it is a health care project, then the project should take advantage of what is known about the particular subject being tested. If it is an education project, principles of learning theory and curriculum development are likely to apply. In other words, sound practices of research, development, and management in the appropriate field must be both used and communicated to the grantmaker. For this reason, during project design, frequently, research will have to be done. For example, a grantseeker may have an idea for a particular testing option but is not sure if it actually will provide the necessary indicators on which to base a project design. The grantseeker reviews literature on the testing technique being considered. A particular tool might be needed, maybe to teach a skill or to construct a structure necessary to the project. This may require research to ensure that the tool fits the use. In analyzing project choices, do your homework. Research the latest advances and other projects in the topic field.

This next point is sometimes hard to implement. Someone has to take charge. At some point, decisions must be made. Many times, there are groups who are very sincere in their desire to develop realistic, workable projects, but no one in the group will make a decision. These organizations develop proposals in which there are committee meetings, advisory meetings, planning sessions, more planning sessions, more meetings . . . and nothing is really done. Unless the grantmaker is specifically letting a planning grant, these projects do not get funded, nor should they. Everyone is busy going to or coming from meetings, so they *think* something is being accomplished, but it is really not. Being busy does not necessarily mean work is getting done. Planning should be a part of every project, but not the beginning, middle, and end of it. This often happens because of a misunderstanding on the part of a grantseeker about what grantmakers are after.

Grantmakers know that grantseekers use their expertise, experience, skill, education, knowledge of precedents, and best guesses to design the best project you can to solve the problem. They also know that an organization cannot guarantee the results. The project is an experiment. What an organization can guarantee is that it will follow the procedures and processes set up in the proposal (the contract with the grantmaker) to the best of its ability. The organization can guarantee that it will do an honest, thorough job. Some projects will not get the result expected—unintended consequences happen. Has the grantmaker necessarily lost on the investment? No, because it has still added to the body of knowledge about the subject matter. The project has illustrated other issues relating to the problem. At the least, you have proven what will not work. Sometimes that knowledge leads your organization or someone else into a better project design that works the second time around.

The bottom line is that to have a fundable project, it must potentially solve the problem your organization and the grantmaker are interested in and must generate results that can be measured in some way. This leads us to the next step in project design—the results.

## Results Are the Goal

Does it do any good to do a project just to do it, because it seems to be a good thing to do? How many programs or projects have been implemented in your community that were here today and gone tomorrow? Have you ever said, "If they'll just quit changing things every other day, we might get something done?" Of course, you have. Why? Because these projects were not well founded. They sounded like a good idea. They were creative and maybe even fun, but they were not valid. They did not work. This book will lead you through a process to help ensure that your project will work—to ensure that your project is designed to get and measure results.

Grantmakers fund projects that have the best chance for positive results. Another word for results is "benefits." Of what benefit is your project to the target population? If your project is not going to benefit anyone, then why do it? Grantmakers have limited funds. They want to put them where they will do the most benefit, and one cannot blame them for that. It is your job to be sure the benefits, the intended results of your project, are clear.

Return to the vandalism example in Exhibit 3.1. The hypothetical project is to initiate a buddy-system teen supervision program involving parents, area businesses and industries, community agencies, and religious leaders. What results are being sought? What should be different after the initial months or years of the project have been completed? What will happen if the project is successful? Whom will the project benefit and how?

Obviously, the main goal is a reduction in the incidence of vandalism. However, there are other benefits. Middle school children should become more positively involved with their parents and in the community. The community should become more cohesive and proactive. Other projects involving a wide range of age groups should spring up. Think about the project. There are many results or benefits that could occur.

Now look at your project idea. Think about the desired results and benefits. Use the benefits worksheet provided in Exhibit 3.5 and on the disk (📁 0303.DOC) to record your thoughts.

## Exhibit 3.5

0303.DOC

### Benefits Worksheet

**Broad Problem:**

Youth vandalism has skyrocketed in the community

**Real Problem(s):**

a) too little parental supervision

b) too little community supervision

**Project Idea**

Write a brief description of your project below.

A buddy-system teen supervision program involving parents, area businesses and industries, community agencies, and religious leaders.

**Results and Benefits**

If your project is successful, what specific results and benefits with regard to the target population can be expected?

1  Reductions in the incidence of vandalism.

2  Middle-school children become more positively involved with their parents and in the community.

3  Commuinity more cohesive and proactive

4  _____

5  _____

6  _____

7  _____

8  _____

# Chapter 4

# Organizing the Project

## *Main Steps—Outlining*

What is an outline? It is simply a way of organizing something in logical, step-by-step order from first to last, or simple to complex. It is not hard and it is not magic, but it is absolutely necessary to further project development and to the eventual writing of the proposal. Almost all projects can be broken down into some core processes. These core processes are as follows:

- Investigate resources.
- Gather necessary tools.
- Put the project together.
- Implement the project.
- Evaluate the project.
- Strategically manage the project.

Apply this to an everyday activity, for example, making peanut butter sandwiches. Everyone knows how to make a peanut butter and jelly sandwich. There may be a few variations, but the principles are the same. What are the main steps? Where does one start?

- Investigate resources. Find out what is in the kitchen and make a grocery list.

  What is the next thing to do? We know we have peanut butter and bread, but no jelly. Of course, you cannot have peanut butter sandwiches without milk, so we need milk. While we were checking out the cabinets, we noticed there were no napkins, we will get some of those too. That leads to the next step.

- Gather necessary tools. Purchase groceries. We now we have peanut butter, jelly, bread, milk, and even napkins. What is next?
- Put the project together. Make the sandwich—lots of peanut butter, lots of jelly, and it has to be on white bread (we do not know why, it is just better that way). A big glass of milk and we are ready.
- Implement the project. Eat the sandwich. Oh boy, nothing like a good peanut butter and jelly sandwich!
- Evaluate the project. How was it? Good sandwich. Have another!
- Strategically manage the project for long-term results. Put the lids back on the jars, twist tie the bread, put the milk in the refrigerator, and wipe the counter.

Look at another example, in Exhibit 4.1. This time, the project is to build a fire. One point should be noted here: One may organize the fire building somewhat differently than this example. Does this mean that there is a right way and a wrong way to organize the building of a fire? Of course not. If the fire gets started safely and accomplishes its task— whether that task is to provide warmth, cook dinner, roast marshmallows, or just to sit around and sing songs—then any organizational scheme is

EXHIBIT **4.1**

## Outline Example: Building a Fire to Cook Marshmallows

   I. Collect materials.
      A. Collect only dry, standing deadwood.
      B. Collect some of all sizes from pencil thin to three inches thick.
  II. Prepare materials.
      A. Break firewood into appropriate lengths.
      B. Sort by size.
 III. Lay and light fire.
      A. Prepare ground site—clear leaves to bare ground and make a circle of rocks.
      B. Lay fire, starting with the smallest pieces and growing in size.
      C. Using no more than two matches, light fire.
 IV. Cleaning up
      A. Separate live embers.
      B. Extinguish fire.
      C. Bury ashes, embers, and partly burned wood.
      D. Spread leaves and leave site cleaner than you found it.

acceptable. The point is not to come up with the correct organization, but to come up with an organization that works.

Alternatives to the methods outlined in Exhibit 4.1 include using an ax instead of one's hands and feet, purchasing at the supermarket, laying the fire in a prepared fire pit, using paper to get the fire going, or using a cigarette lighter for flame.

None of this truly matters. What does matter is that you think through an organized, step-by-step way of getting the job done. The particulars of the organization are not what are important. The fact that the job is organized at all is what is important.

## ORGANIZE YOUR PROJECT—AN EXERCISE

 0401.DOC

### Step Eleven: Write Down the Main Steps  0401.DOC

Think through your project. What are the five or six or seven main steps? Use the templates provided on the disk to record your answers. Put steps in logical, first-to-last order. There may be some steps that happen at the same time. In this case, it does not matter which one is before the other. Do not forget project setup, management, and evaluation.

Look back at your list. If you could not get your list down to five or six, then are any of your steps really substeps that belong under a broader step? Work with these main steps until you are satisfied that you have captured the essence of your project. Again, be sure you have included project setup, management, and evaluation.

### Step Twelve: Write Down the Key Activities to Accomplish the Main Steps

 0401.DOC

Go back to our examples. First, look at the peanut butter sandwich. Here are the main steps again.

- Investigate resources (what is in the pantry?).
- Purchase grocery items (get what is needed).
- Put the project together (make the sandwich).
- Implement the project (eat the sandwich).
- Evaluate the project (was it good?).
- Manage the project (clean up).

What are the actual activities we have to do, in the order in which we must do them, to accomplish the main steps? Take each one individually.

I. Investigate resources (what is in the pantry?).
   A. Check for peanut butter.
      1. Look in the cupboard.
      2. If found, open container and check amount in jar.
   B. Check for jelly.
      1. Look in the refrigerator for grape jelly.
      2. If found, open container and check amount in jar.
   C. Check for milk.
      1. Look in the refrigerator for milk.
      2. Open container and apply the sniff test—is it fresh and is there enough?
   D. Check for bread.
      1. Look in breadbox for white bread.
      2. Check for mold.
   E. Make a list of things needed.

II. Purchase grocery items (get what is needed).
   A. Prepare to go to the grocery store and drive to store.
      1. Get checkbook.
      2. Take car to grocery store.
      3. Get car keys.
      4. Open garage.
      5. Back out and take Main Street to grocery.
   B. Shop for needed items.
      1. Load cart.
      2. Pay cashier.
      3. Load groceries in car.
   C. Drive home.
      1. Start car.
      2. Take Main Street home.
      3. Enter garage.
      4. Close garage door.
   D. Unload groceries and carry them to the kitchen.

III. Put the project together (make the sandwich).

    A. Open containers and prepare food.

        1. Open peanut butter jar.

        2. Open grape jelly jar.

        3. Get out two slices of bread.

    B. Get out tools.

        1. Get two knives.

        2. Get out napkin.

    C. Make the sandwich.

        1. With one knife, spread peanut butter on one slice of bread.

        2. With the other knife, spread jelly on the other slice of bread.

        3. Put the two pieces of bread together with the peanut butter and jelly sides together.

        4. Put the sandwich on a napkin.

    D. Get liquid refreshment to go with sandwich.

        1. Get a drinking glass.

        2. Get milk from the refrigerator, open, and pour into glass.

IV. Implement the project (eat the sandwich).

    A. Prepare a place to eat sandwich.

        1. Carry sandwich and milk to table beside favorite chair.

        2. Sit in chair and put feet up on ottoman.

    B. Consume sandwich and milk.

        1. Pick up sandwich and take a bite; chew and swallow.

        2. Drink some milk.

        3. Continue steps C and D until both the sandwich and milk have been consumed.

V. Evaluate the project (was it good?).

    A. Has hunger ceased?

    B. Is there a pleasant memory of the experience?

    C. Is there a good taste in the mouth?

    D. Is there a desire for another?

    E. Is the event worth repeating?

    F. Were the desired results achieved?

VI. Manage the project (clean up).
  A. Go into the kitchen.
  B. Put up containers of food.
    1. Put the lids back on the jars.
    2. Put the peanut butter in the cabinet.
    3. Put the jelly in the refrigerator.
    4. Put the cap on the milk.
    5. Put the milk in the refrigerator.
  C. Throw away the napkin.
  D. Wipe the counter.

Making a peanut butter and jelly sandwich has a lot of activities. It is important to point out one fact—this outline was created without actually creating and eating peanut butter sandwiches. The project was thought through and planned out in an office without a refrigerator. People are often hesitant to try to plan a project for a number of reasons, the most prominent being, "We don't have all the information we need." Notice that we did not have all the information we needed either. We did not know if there was peanut butter or jelly already available or if the milk was sour (it was). We built the investigation of the availability of resources into the project. Not knowing a few things does not matter. A project step to investigate those things should be included. You still should be able to imagine the rest of the steps in the project. Just close your eyes and imagine what you would do if you had the money and someone said you had to begin the project tomorrow.

Look at an outline of a more serious project about establishing a counseling program.

  I. Establish a counseling center.
   A. Staff the counseling center.
     1. Advertise positions.
     2. Advisory board interviews of applicants.
   B. House the counseling center—renovate building.
     1. Draw up detailed plans.
     2. Solicit volunteer services for construction.

 II. Enroll students.
   A. Survey and test potential participants.
     1. Compose survey and test and validate.
     2. Implement survey.

B. Register students.
1. Parent and student orientation.
2. Schedule entry.

III. Execute counseling program.
A. Implement and document sessions.
1. Schedule.
2. Develop counseling report.
B. Evaluate progress.
1. Set up counselor, parent, and student review.
2. Implement reviews.

IV. Monitor counseling program.
A. Advisory committee.
1. Plan review procedures.
2. Plan communications.
B. Manage program.
1. Set up supervision system.
2. Set up reporting system.

For the time being, leave your outline in this stage, with the major steps identified, and some of the activities or substeps written in. The outline will be completed later, when the project outline is expanded. This will be done in Part III.

## PROJECT PROFILE—AN EXERCISE

 0402.DOC

At this point, there should be enough general information to create a project profile and search for a potential funder. Exhibit 4.2 can act as a guide through this process. This project profile will be your most important tool once you begin searching for the federal, state, foundation, and corporate grants.

Create project profile:

**1.** The Broad Problem—identify
**2.** The Real Problem—identify
**3.** The Target Population—identify
**4.** A Project Synopsis—a good, solid project idea. No need to be formal here—just an overview.

EXHIBIT **4.2**

## Project Profile Worksheet

Broad Problem

Real Problem(s)

Target Population

Project Synopsis

_____
_____
_____
_____
_____
_____
_____
_____
_____
_____
_____
_____
_____
_____
_____
_____
_____
_____

Equipment Needs

| Equipment | Guestimated Cost |
|---|---|
| | |
| | |
| | |
| | |
| | |
| | |
| | |

## Materials Needs

| Materials | Guestimated Cost |
|---|---|
|  |  |
|  |  |
|  |  |
|  |  |
|  |  |
|  |  |
|  |  |
|  |  |

## People Needs

| People | Guestimated Cost |
|---|---|
|  |  |
|  |  |
|  |  |
|  |  |
|  |  |
|  |  |
|  |  |
|  |  |

## Supplies Needs

| Supplies | Guestimated Cost |
|---|---|
|  |  |
|  |  |
|  |  |
|  |  |
|  |  |
|  |  |
|  |  |
|  |  |

*Continued*

**EXHIBIT 4.2** *Continued*

Facilities Needs

| Facilities | Guestimated Cost |
|---|---|
|  |  |
|  |  |
|  |  |
|  |  |
|  |  |
|  |  |
|  |  |
|  |  |

Duration of Project in Years or Parts of Years

Approximate Funding Needed

Potential Project Partners

| Organization | Address | Contact | Job Function |
|---|---|---|---|
|  |  |  |  |
|  |  |  |  |
|  |  |  |  |
|  |  |  |  |
|  |  |  |  |
|  |  |  |  |
|  |  |  |  |
|  |  |  |  |

**5.** Equipment Needed

Make a list of any of the tools that will be needed to effectively accomplish the project. Be very careful—no extraneous equipment! Just list the kinds of equipment needed to do the project. This is not the place to record your whole wish list!

**6.** Materials Needed

Does the organization need a lot of texts, reference materials, or software to accomplish the project? If significant material is needed, make a list. What about research and testing materials?

**7.** People Needed

What additional staff or volunteers will be needed to accomplish the project?

**8.** Supplies Needed

Is this a paper-intensive project? Will you need maintenance supplies?

**9.** Facilities Needed

Are you going to need building renovation? Will you have to rent?

**10.** Duration in Years or Parts of Years

Remember, you are estimating the time until you have provable results to present to the funder. Will this be in six months, a couple of years, or more?

**11.** Funding Needed

Look over your notes here. Estimate the amount of funds you will need from the funder. Remember, the funder will not cover all the project costs, so subtract a portion for your contribution.

**12.** Potential Project Partners

Will you have partners on your project? It is to your advantage. Partners indicate to the funder that the project is that much more solid—it has more people watching over it to ensure its success.

A few sentences concisely describing each of the twelve elements in a Project Profile should be sufficient. After completion of the Project Profile, it is time to begin searching for a matching funder.

# How to Find a Funder to Match Your Project

# Chapter 5

# Introduction to Finding Funders

Researching funding sources to support solutions for problems is a time-consuming activity, and it can be confusing if an organization does not know where to look. There are many avenues for finding sources but few guides to help work through the myriad types of information available.

As discussed in Section I, it is very important to focus on a particular problem, then design a project to solve that problem before attempting to research funding sources. There are so many sources, all saying they support health care, education, the arts, or some other general topic, that one can be lulled into thinking that all that is necessary is to write a "give-me-letter" to each one and voila! The money just rolls in. If it were that easy, everyone would have many programs supported with grant funds.

Grants acquisition is highly competitive. Those that succeed recognized the importance of knowing everything possible about a funder that is to be approached. However, each and every funder that purports to support education cannot be researched before submitting a proposal. It would take years to do that and a proposal would never get in the mail. The prospects can be narrowed down through savvy research.

Grants can be thought of as originating from four basic sources: the federal government, foundations, corporations or companies, and state and local sources. While many of the basics of grantseeking remain the same, each source takes a slightly different approach.

Each source funds in different ways and with different motives. Deciding which of the four grant sources to pursue is part of the matching process.

Where does this research fit in our grants acquisition process? This section provides step-by-step processes for researching and matching foundation, government, and corporate funders.

## *The Total Grants Acquisition Process*

The process of grantseeking and proposal writing is complex. Most mistakes made by novice grantseekers are due to the false assumption that writing the proposal is the focus of the process. Actually, developing something to write about is the key. In the case of a grant proposal, that "something" is a project, complete with a start, a finish, and activities in between. Writing the proposal is only 15 to 20 percent of the entire process. Exhibit 5.1 illustrates the grants acquisition process.

### EXHIBIT 5.1

### Grants Acquisition Process

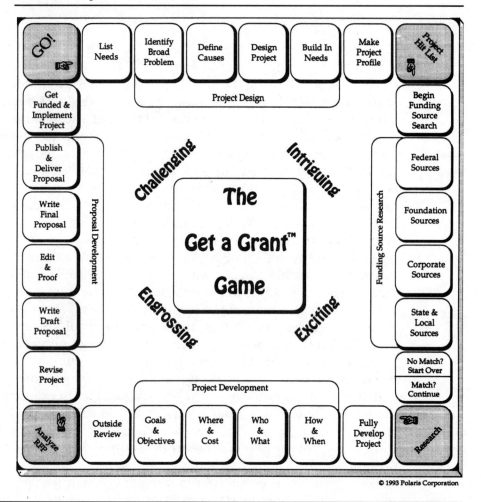

© 1993 Polaris Corporation

Grantseeking begins with project design—define a problem and create a project to solve it. Next comes funding source research—find a grantor with program aims that match your organization, problem, and project. Next comes project development—take your project idea and flesh it out into a fully developed project. Last comes proposal development—from your developed project, a proposal is written. Many proposals can be written from one project, but each proposal is used once for a specific grantor.

## The Concept of Match

To have a successful, ongoing grants effort, it is important to have a number of projects in process, into the design phase, at all times. Project profiles should be kept handy for review when that request for proposal (RFP) arrives on August 1 with a deadline of August 20. With the information gathered during project design, and the knowledge of how to analyze the RFP and complete the project development, an organization should be able to meet the deadline with a competitive project and proposal.

In addition, and more importantly, if the entire staff is involved in project design, there is an ongoing team effort in planning and implementing changes that improve services or products for the target population. Designing the projects elicits change in and of itself as the focus changes from routine and status quo to a problem-solving atmosphere.

Finally, and more to the point at this stage of the book, project profiles are needed if finding funders for projects is going to be actively pursued. The information gained in the design process is needed to find a matching funder.

What are you looking for in a match? There are many clues.

## Match the Problem

As discussed thoroughly in Section I, a project must address a problem in which the funder is intensely interested.

## Eligibility

An organization must be eligible for funding by the grantmaker. This is both a legal and a policy issue.

## Legal Issue

Both donations to and grants from a grantmaker have tax implications. Grantmakers are themselves nonprofit organizations or are for-profit corporations with a grant program that affords a tax break. The grantmaker pays no taxes on the funds granted. If the grantmaker receives donations, people making donations pay no taxes on the funds donated. As with any tax-related issue, an extensive body of law governs the process. Grantmakers must donate to organizations with the appropriate tax status or be themselves required to pay taxes on the funds they have donated.

Most organizations eligible for grant funding are classified as 501(c)(3) organizations. An organization may qualify for tax-exempt 501(c)(3) status if it is organized and operated exclusively for one or more of the following purposes: charitable, religious, educational, scientific, literary, testing for public safety, fostering national or international amateur sports competition, or the prevention of cruelty to children or animals. The organization must be a corporation, community chest, fund, or foundation to qualify.

Examples of qualifying organizations are nonprofit old age homes, parent–teacher associations, charitable hospitals or other charitable organizations, alumni associations, schools, chapters of the Red Cross or Salvation Army, boy's and girl's clubs, and churches. A state or municipal instrumentality may qualify if it is organized as a separate entity from the governmental unit that created it and if it otherwise meets the organizational and operational tests of section 501(c)(3). Examples of qualifying instrumentalities might include state schools, universities, or hospitals.

An organization may be tax exempt, however, and not be a 501(c)(3) organization. Public schools are 509(a) organizations. They are tax exempt, but many grantmakers will not give to anything other than a 501(c)(3), thus eliminating public schools who have not set up a 501(c)(3) foundation from which to seek grant funding. If an organization is not a 501(c)(3), the advantages of becoming one should be considered.

The process has two basic steps. Step one is to create a not-for-profit corporation under the laws of the organization's state. Step two is to apply for 501(c)(3) tax-exempt status from the Internal Revenue Service.

Creating a not-for-profit corporation, in most states, is done through the state's Secretary of State's office. In some states, a lawyer must be used to create and file the appropriate paperwork. In other states, an individual may file all the paperwork without the assistance of a lawyer. If a lawyer's assistance is required, the time the lawyer spends establishing the not-for-profit corporation may become a tax-exempt donation by the lawyer to the organization once the 501(c)(3) tax-exempt status is obtained.

Application to the Internal Revenue Service for 501(c)(3) tax-exempt status is done using IRS Form 1023. The form contains instructions and checklists to help provide the information needed to process an application. Additional important information is found in IRS Publication 557, "Tax-Exempt Status for Your Organization."

### Policy Issue

A grantmaker sets up policies concerning which organizations it will make awards to and which ones it will not. One grantmaker may have a policy that it will fund only religious schools, or rural health organizations, or arts programs in a certain county of a state. These policies rarely change. Some are stated clearly in the published blurb in a Foundation Center directory, and some are not so clearly stated. As a grantseeker, one must read between the lines. Look at what the grantmaker has funded. If the grantmaker says, among other things, that it funds programs in the arts, but in its five years of existence has never funded an arts program, what should that tell you? Their program should be looked at closely. If a grantmaker publishes that it funds arts programs, but on looking at the list of funded grants you notice that the only arts program listed is Picasso Bill's Art Gallery, then what chance do you have? Read between the lines.

***Location.*** The preponderance of foundations fund programs only within a defined area of the country, usually within a city or a few counties in a state. Therefore, the closer you are to the foundation's location, the better chance you have. A number of larger foundations do fund programs nationally and internationally. The federal government funds programs nationally and internationally. Corporations are like foundations. They tend to fund programs close to their locations—programs that benefit their employees. Some corporations sponsor special nationwide competitions.

***Scope and Amount.*** Grant funders tend to specialize in programs of a certain size and scope. The grant amounts awarded are published amounts—they are a part of the public record. One funder may tend to fund $100,000 and greater programs that are regional in scope, whereas another may fund programs from $500 to $25,000 of more highly targeted scope, serving a more specialized target population being served over a limited area of a county. An organization's project scope and the amount of money it needs should closely match the track record and published focus of the grantmaker. In other words, if the project requires a $10,000 investment, do not apply to a grantmaker who tends to fund $1,000 programs. Surprisingly, one also would not go to a grantmaker who tends to fund $100,000 programs. The organization's investment need should be closer to the average amount the funder tends to award.

## HOW TO FIND THE MATCH?—AN EXERCISE

 0501.DOC

A great deal of thought and careful study by professional grantseekers has been synthesized into steps that, if followed, should provide the information needed to effectively research a matching funder and then approach that funder to invest in your project. With each step, there is guiding information and there may be a worksheet to help you record the facts you glean from the process.

### Choose a Logical Starting Point

Use logical reasoning, and the information known about the project, to pick a type of funding with which to start. Here are some examples.

- If your project will serve people in a large area (a state or region), start your research with federal programs and then progress to national-level foundations.
- If your project can be a model program throughout the nation for other organizations like yours, start your research with federal programs and national-level foundations.
- If the project can only be a model program for those in your state and does not readily apply to others in the nation, start with state foundations and state and local sources.
- If the project relates specifically to improving services to your community, start with local corporations and local foundations.

### Get Help

Involve your colleagues. As previously stated, finding funding sources, if done right, is time consuming, but it is one of the easiest parts of the process to pass on to a team member. Develop a research plan, using the form on the disk, and ask several people to be responsible for some part of the research. There is a place for someone who likes to surf the Net and for someone who likes to research with books. There is a place for someone who is good at follow-up and details. Read through the steps necessary for researching each type of funder in the pages that follow and see who would be a good research assistant.

School personnel can enlist the aid of parent association members, students, library–media personnel, and teachers (and their spouses), as well as interested community supporters. Health care organizations can add tasks for their volunteers, for community supporters, and for research assistants. Nonprofits can also make use of volunteer organizations and community support groups, as well as beneficiaries of their services. People are retiring young with many productive years ahead of them. Many have related expertise in management or organizational development. This wonderful community resource can be tapped into by contacting organizations of retired persons and even by running ads in the newspaper.

# Chapter 6

# Researching Federal Funding Sources

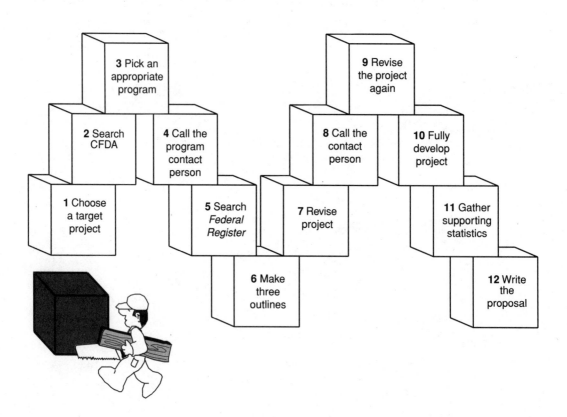

# Introduction

For grantseeking purposes, federal funding sources are divided into two main categories: (1) formula grant programs, and (2) project grant programs.

Briefly, according to the federal government, formula grant programs are "allocations of money to states or their subdivisions in accordance with a distribution formula prescribed by law or administrative regulation for activities of a continuing nature not confined to a specific purpose." In education, the Title I program is a formula grant program. The money granted in a formula program goes to a state or other governmental agency, which allocates funds to local organizations by formula. The state agency, under certain circumstances, can keep a portion of this formula money for project grants. One would then write a proposal to the state agency, not directly to the federal source. In the field of social services, the food stamp program is supported by a formula grant program. Formula grant funds can fund regular, day-to-day programs if those programs serve the target population for which they were intended.

Project grant funds provide competitive funding to selected organizations proposing a project that solves the problem at issue with the particular federal group (program) offering the funding. "Winners" of project grants are selected through a competitive review process.

Project grant money from the federal government is meant to "fill gaps" and to "supplement, not supplant." Federal project grant money is not meant to and will not fund regular, day-to-day programs. To get federal project grant money, a project must be creative and innovative and solve a real problem.

When reviewing the recommended catalogs and directories of funding sources, look for project grants for which your organization is eligible. If a formula program is identified that addresses the same issues addressed by your project, contact the state representative for that program and see if there is money set aside for competitive project grant funds allocated by the state.

Eligibility is a critical issue in deciding whether to puruse a given funding source. In education, there will normally be a note that local education agencies (LEAs), state education agencies (SEAs), or institutes of higher education (IHEs) are eligible. A school or school district is an LEA. SEAs are agencies such as state departments of education. Another type of eligibility is "nonprofit" or "not-for-profit." Public schools and many private schools, as well as many health care and social service organizations are nonprofit and therefore eligible for funding. Remember, however, there may be further specification of a particular type or eligibility according to tax-exempt status such as 501(c)(3). Talk to a contact person for the funding source to determine for sure whether the organization is eligible to receive grant funding.

For some programs, your organization is not directly eligible. Do not eliminate these programs if they closely match your objectives. Find an organization that is eligible for the funds and partner with them on your project.

## Research Steps

### Step One: Choose a Target Project

Funders want to fund innovative, well-developed projects that are designed to solve problems for your service population. To have a successful grants effort, projects should be developed continually, as problems are identified, much as they were in Chapter 4. (See  0402.DOC)

What issues are addressed by your project? Make a list on the sheet provided in Exhibit 6.1 or on the disk ( 0601.DOC). This list will help expedite the search for funders. Here are some examples for guidance.

---

**EXAMPLE PROJECT** *Implement a Community Senior Watch Network for Visiting, Assisting, and Referring Senior Citizens*

Issues: Senior Citizens, Community Development, Volunteers, Health Care, Referral Network, Improvement of Quality of Life, Crime Prevention

---

**EXAMPLE PROJECT** *Develop a High Interest–Low Vocabulary Reading Program for Middle School Students with a Two-to-Four Grade Level Reading Deficit*

Issues: Curriculum Development, Middle School Students, Reading, Basic Skills, Literacy, Development of Teaching Materials, Drop-out Prevention, Motivation

---

**EXAMPLE PROJECT** *Perform a Study of Menopausal Women to Determine Whether Hormone Replacement Therapy Increases Incidence of Breast Cancer*

Issues: Health Care, Women, Study, Prevention

---

EXHIBIT 6.1  0601.DOC

## Issues Worksheet

Broad Problem

Real Problem(s)

Project Synopsis

Issues Addressed

1. _____
2. _____
3. _____
4. _____
5. _____
6. _____
7. _____
8. _____
9. _____
10. _____

### *Step Two: Search the Catalog of Federal Domestic Assistance*

 0602.DOC

The Catalog of Federal Domestic Assistance (CFDA)

is a government-wide compendium of Federal programs, projects, services, and activities which provide assistance or benefits to the American public. It contains financial and nonfinancial assistance programs administered by departments and establishments of the Federal Government.

As the basic reference source of Federal programs, the primary purpose of the Catalog is to assist users in identifying programs which meet specific objectives of the potential applicant . . . .

*Introduction, Catalog of Federal Domestic Assistance*

The Catalog, as it is known by grantseekers, contains an extensive profile of all funding the U.S. government provides domestically. Yes, *all*. It is not necessary to look to any other source for a complete rundown. Other sources do provide supplementary advantage for you in your grantseeking; however, the CFDA should be your primary resource. Any public library will have a copy of the CFDA. In addition, university libraries and other grantseekers are likely to have copies for use as a reference.

The profiles in the CFDA are of the primary funding source. Each primary grant program described in the Catalog can have many subprograms. In other words, there is a large pot of money allocated for a stated purpose as described in the CFDA. Within that large pot of money, many smaller project grant programs may exist and change from year to year. If the problem addressed by that overall program is the same as, or similar to, the one addressed by your project, then it is worth further research to see if there is a more specific project grant program with which your project fits.

Considering the amount of information within, the CFDA is an inexpensive publication at around $50 per year. This includes the basic, loose-leaf manual and one update mailed six months after the publishing of the basic manual.

---

*To order the CFDA*

Call the U.S. Government Printing Office, 202-783-3238 with a MasterCard or Visa number

or

Write the Superintendent of Documents, U.S. Government Printing Office, Washington, D.C., 20402, and include a check or money order.

*Strategies for Searching the Catalog of Federal Domestic Assistance*

1. First, look at the Subjects Worksheet for Exhibit 6.2 of the subject list. Check all those topics that relate to your project problem and process. Include any topic that is logically related in any way.

2. Next, look at the Functions Worksheet and check all those topics that pertain to your project. See Exhibit 6.3.

3. Open the CFDA to the Subject Index. In the space provided, record the CFDA numbers of the subjects matching the items you checked on the Subjects Worksheet.

## EXHIBIT 6.2

## Step Two—CFDA Research Worksheets

Which of the following topics could match the issues embraced by your project? Put a check beside each matching topic.

### Subjects Worksheet

☐ Academic facilities

☐ Accident prevention

☐ Addition

☐ Adult education

☐ Advanced technology

☐ Aeronautics

☐ Aid to Families with Dependent Children

☐ Age discrimination

☐ Aging and the aged

☐ Agriculture commodities

☐ Agriculture labor

☐ Agriculture loans

☐ Agriculture research

☐ Agriculture stabilization

☐ AIDS

☐ Braille

☐ Broadcasting

☐ Business development

☐ Cancer research

☐ Cardio-vascular system research

☐ Career education

☐ Child abuse and neglect

☐ Child development

☐ Child health

☐ Child welfare

☐ Children, disabled

☐ Children, education

☐ Citizenship education

☐ Civil defense

☐ Civil rights

☐ Consumers

☐ Contagious diseases

☐ Controlled substances

☐ Cooperative housing

☐ Corrections

(For a complete listing see  0602.DOC)

## EXHIBIT 6.3

### Step Two—Search the CFDA, continued

Which of the following topics could match the issues embraced by your project? Put a check beside each matching topic.

**Functional Worksheet**

☐ Academic Facilities      ☐ Food and Nutrition

☐ Agriculture      ☐ Health

☐ Business and Commerce      ☐ Housing

☐ Community Development      ☐ Income Security and Social Services

☐ Consumer Protection      ☐ Information and Statistics

☐ Cultural Affairs      ☐ Law, Justice, and Legal Services

☐ Disaster Prevention and Relief      ☐ Natural Resources

☐ Education      ☐ Regional Development

☐ Employment, Labor, Training      ☐ Science and Technology

☐ Energy      ☐ Transportation

☐ Environmental Quality

4. Now, turn to the Functional Index Summary in the CFDA. In the space provided, record the CFDA numbers of the functional areas that match your areas of interest.

5. Turn in the CFDA to the Added Programs Index. Make a list of the programs (and their CFDA numbers) that appear to match your project issues.

6. Turn in the CFDA to the Deleted Programs Index. Check the lists you have made on the previous pages to see if any of the programs you chose have been deleted. Eliminate them from your list(s).

7. Look up each CFDA profile you identified. Fill out the charts in the CFDA Research Form for each CFDA profile you analyze. 📁 0603.DOC

8. Review your charts from your research so far. Pick one or two programs that seem to match your project best. Look at the program entry under "Related Programs." Listed related programs on your Research Form.

9. Look up the related program(s) and analyze them for eligibility and applicability. Use the CFDA Research Form to record your notes.

### Step Three: Pick Programs to Target  0603.DOC

Review the programs you chose as having the best fit with your organization and project. Review the related programs you identified. Which one or two programs best fit your organization and project? Enter the appropriate information into the CFDA Contact Sheet provided. These targeted programs are the ones on which you will seek further information.

### Step Four: Call the Program Contact Person

Using the Interview Guide provided, call the program contact person and gather the information indicated. Make a copy of the Interview Guide for each CFDA program you want to research. Remember, we are just providing a guide to help you initiate the conversation. The resulting discussion depends on the answers given and further questions asked.

Here is what you will ask and why:

I am calling in reference to the _____ program. I am (name), (title), (organization). We are a (describe your organization). Are we eligible to apply for a grant under your program?

You are only checking eligibility. In the CFDA program profile, there will be information about eligible organizations, but it is very important to check to be sure you are directly eligible because you do not want to spend hours and hours developing your project and writing a proposal when you have no chance of being awarded funds. You are not describing your project, just your organization type. You might say, "We are a 501(c)(3) community foundation," or "We are a public high school," or "We are a for-profit clinic partnered with a nonprofit social service agency," or "We are a county government agency." The program contact person may ask additional questions about how your organization is organized or to whom it reports to determine eligibility.

- When will an RFP be let on this program? When will a notice appear in the *Federal Register*? (The *Federal Register* will be discussed in the next few pages.)

The program contact person will give you specific information about upcoming programs, if those programs are imminent. Many programs are let about the same time every year, so the contact person will tell you to look in the October issues of the *Federal Register* or the third week in May or whatever period may be appropriate to find the notice.

- When did the RFP come out during last year's cycle? When did a notice appear in the *Federal Register*?

If there is not a current cycle or there will not be one for some months, ask when the notice came out last year. Libraries keep back issues of the *Federal Register*. It will help you understand the goals of the program and the information they request if you read the past notice(s). Programs do not change drastically from year to year, so you can get a head start by beginning your project development, gathering your information, and making your plans. The program contact person will likely direct you to an Internet site where you can download the RFP and required forms. If you do not have access to the Internet, go to your local public library and ask your reference librarian to provide assistance. Local colleges and universities have access, and you may be able to use their libraries to acquire the information you need.

- May I have a copy of the RFP (*current* or *last year's if the current one has not been published*)?

If there is not a current RFP, ask if you can get a copy of the last one. Many times, the proposal requirements do not change significantly. Looking at last year's RFP, you can determine general program goals, areas of concentration, important parts of the project to emphasize, marketing points, and many other pieces of information. You can see how stringent the proposal requirements are, so you can estimate how many hours it will take to complete your project development and proposal writing.

- Do you have a past, successful proposal for us to use as a guide? We will be glad to pay for duplicating costs.

Some programs will provide a copy of a past successful proposal, if you would like to have some further guidance. This is not helpful because every project and every writer's style is so different and there is nothing that can or should be copies, but people in workshops indicate a desire to have a proposal to review.

- Other questions (write them out in advance).

If, in the review of the program profile, there are other questions, write them down and prepare to ask them during this conversation. Be careful, though. Do not ask questions that are already clearly answered in the profile. In other words, read the profile carefully so the time of the program contact person is not wasted.

This leads to another point. Never, ever call anyone (except maybe your Aunt Sarah) without first preparing for your call. Be sure you know the purpose for the call, questions you want to ask, and the desired result. Everyone should have to listen to a couple of hours of call-in radio. Even though people supposedly know why they are calling, they hem and haw and stumble and ramble so much, it is a surprise that the hosts do not just summarily cut them all off the air. When you make a business phone call, keep this in mind. If you are not prepared, you are guilty of theft. Yes, theft. You are stealing the most precious thing a person has— his or her time. Once lost, it cannot be regained. Know why you are calling. Do your homework so that you do not ask questions you could have found the answers to on your own. Ask your questions, make your statements, and then politely end the call with a thank you. The program coordinator (and everyone else) will love you for it. You want to make a good impression. You do not want to be remembered as, "Oh, no, it's that organization where that lady (or man) rambles on and on and says nothing."

### Step Five: Search through the **Federal Register**

Each Federal working day, the *Federal Register* publishes current Presidential proclamations and Executive orders, Federal agency regulations having general applicability and legal effect, proposed agency rules, and documents that are required by statute to be published.

*The United States Government Manual*

The *Federal Register* can be found in public libraries, university libraries, and private libraries of other grantseekers. Alternately, the *Federal Register* can be purchased for around $500 a year or half that for six months. If you subscribe to the *Federal Register*, you will receive a complete document for each day the Federal government works.

---

*To order the* Federal Register

Call 202-783-3238 with a MasterCard or VISA number

or

Write the Superintendent of Documents, U.S. Government Printing Office, Washington, D.C., 29402, and enclose a check or money order.

---

### *Strategies for Searching the* Federal Register

1. Go to the month in which the program contact person said a notice of the program appeared. Look in the monthly index in the front and find the name of the program and page number.

2. Copy the notice. Add the notice to your project/proposal development information. We suggest you make a tabbed notebook in which to organize your research information and responses to the worksheets provided in this book.

3. Every month, an index is published with the happenings of the past calendar year to date. If you are not sure which week or even month a notice appeared, then use the monthly indexes to help you find the notice.

### Step Six: After Receiving the Request for Proposal (RFP), Make Three Outlines

Make three outlines: a Proposal Content Outline, a Publishing Requirements Outline, and a Sales Points or Hot Buttons Outline. This is perhaps the most critical step in the whole grants process. Many people fail to provide the grantmaker a responsive proposal simply because they have left out this step. Because of the importance of making the outlines, a whole section of this book has been written to the issue of analyzing the funder's guidelines or RFP. Section III covers the entire analysis process, including how to make the three outlines.

### Step Seven: Revise the Project and Rewrite the Description  0604.DOC

We started researching federal sources just after we finished our initial project design. It has been a while now since we have taken a critical look at the project. In the meantime, a lot of valuable information has been gained about the federal program we have targeted. We have made our outlines, so we know more about the requirements and interests of the program originators.

Review all the information you have gathered so far, concentrating on the Proposal Content Outline and the Sales Points Outline. Are there things that should be changed about your project to ensure a better fit with the funder? We are not talking about the basic premises, but about smaller details.

Does the funder require a large number of partnerships? Suppose your current project has one or two but could be expanded to include others. Would you not have a better fit with a project expansion? What you are looking for is project improvements based on what you know about the targeted funder. Like a carpenter planing a board, you are fine tuning to make a tight fit.

Use the worksheet provided on the disk to record your ideas for improvements. Then, in the space provided, write a draft project description that includes your project revisions.

### Step Eight: Call the Contact Person Again  0605.DOC

You have come a long way in the grants process and it is likely that you have some questions about the grant program and your project fit. If so, carefully think through what you need to know and write down your questions just as we did for you earlier. After you have written out your questions, then look back over the information you already have and be sure none of your questions have been answered in the literature already provided by the funder. You do not want to call the contact person just to be calling.

Your questions may be about how to prepare the proposal or they may be project oriented. If you are not sure of a fit, give the contact person a very brief (two minutes maximum—practice!) synopsis of your project and ask directly if this project sounds like a fit. Don't expect a direct, "Yes, send it in, it's a winner!" The program contact person may say, "It sounds like a possibility, but be sure you understand that your partnerships must be working partnerships and not just name only arrangements." Or the contact person may say, "Be careful, we don't fund a lot of equipment with this project and it sounds like your project is very equipment heavy." Listen. This conversation is about the contact person's talking to you, not you talking to the contact person. Important information can be gained every time you listen to a program contact person if you will use as few words as possible while you talk. Take notes on what you hear.

Program contact people are intensely interested in receiving proposals for good, solid projects. They are not there to trick you or lead you astray. Their jobs depend on funding good projects and usually they are extremely helpful if you respect their time and expertise.

Use the Contact Form provided on the disk to write down your questions and record the answers.

### Step Nine: Revise the Project Again

Use the guidance of the contact person gained in Step Eight to further revise your project, if necessary. Make a list of the things about your project that you need to change/add/delete to make the project fit the funder's requirements and hot buttons. Revise your project profile to match your revisions. 🖫 0604.DOC

At this point, you should know for sure whether the program is a fit with your project. If so, you are ready for the next steps of the grants process. If not, then go back to Step One, Researching Federal Funding Sources, and start over with another program; or move on to foundation or corporate funders and use the steps we outline to find the match. If you have a project match after completing Step Nine, you are ready to fully develop the project.

# Chapter 7

# Researching Foundation Funding Sources

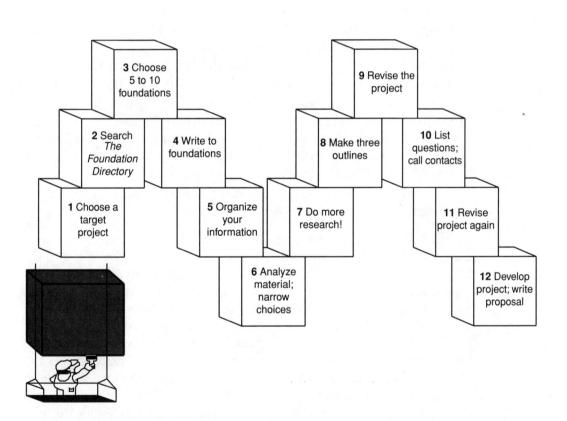

# *Introduction*

> A foundation is a "nongovernmental, nonprofit organization having principal fund of own, managed by its own trustees and directors, established to maintain or aid charitable, educational, religious, or other activities serving public good primarily by making grants to nonprofit organizations. . . ."
>
> *Tax Reform Act, 1969*

There are four types of foundations.

1. *Independent foundation.* This is the foundation you normally think of approaching—the Ford Foundation (refers to the Ford family), Duke Endowment, Pew Charitable Trusts, Kellogg, and others fit into this category.

2. *Company-sponsored foundation.* Many companies sponsor a foundation that is separate from the company but still closely aligned with company interests. The Xerox Foundation, the Avon Foundation, and the MacDonalds Foundation fit into this category. Companies may have a giving program in addition to the foundation.

3. *Community foundation.* These foundations are focused on the community in which they are located. The largest growth in foundations in general is in community foundations. These foundations fund only projects that directly benefit the community.

4. *Operating foundation.* These foundations fund only programs they administer directly and do not accept outside applications.

The Foundation Center is the most authoritative source of information on foundation philanthropy, nonprofit technical assistance, and research. The Foundation Center publishes the definitive directories of foundations in both printed and database versions. The three publications, *The National Data Book of Foundations*, *The Foundation Directory*, and *The Foundation Grants Index*, are the place to start research on foundations. The Foundation Center maintains collections of publications and information at over 100 libraries, in what they call Cooperating Collections. Many public libraries have *The Foundation Directory*, at least, if not the whole collection. Ask the reference librarian. Universities and other grantseekers are also sources of Foundation Center publications.

*The Foundation Center*

79 Fifth Avenue, New York, NY, 10003-3050; phone 212-620-4230

## RESEARCH STEPS—AN EXERCISE

 0701.DOC–0703.DOC

### Step One: Choose a Target Project

Review your project "hit list." This has been said before, but it bears repeating. Funders want to fund innovative, well-developed projects that are designed to solve problems for your service population. To have a successful grants effort, projects should be developed continually, as problems are identified. Project profile sheets should be completed on each project. A template for a project profile is included on the disk, in file 0402.DOC.

### Step Two: *Search* The Foundation Directory

 0701.DOC

Refer to the Introduction to this section for information about The Foundation Center and its publications. There are other directories; however, the Foundation Center directories are the best ones with which to start.

Based on the profiles in the Directory, make a list of the foundations closest in proximity to your location that have interests and that most closely match your target project. Then look at the other states. Entries are organized from largest foundations to smaller foundations in each state section. Read the entries on the largest foundations in other states to see if those foundations give outside the state—in your area. These large national foundations are also potential funders for your projects.

Use the worksheet provided on the disk for guidance and to record your answers.

### Step Three: Choose Five to Ten Foundations

Review the information recorded from your foundation research. Use your Contact Form in Exhibit 7.1 and the disk in file 0605.doc to list pertinent information on each.

### Step Four: Write to the Foundations You Have Chosen

Use the letter in Exhibit 7.2 to set up a template for a form letter to request information from the foundations you have chosen.

### Step Five: Organize Your Information

You can organize the information you obtain on foundations in many ways. File folders, boxes, and stacks are the most rudimentary methods.

### EXHIBIT 7.1

 0605.DOC

## Contact Form

| | |
|---|---|
| Primary Contact Person | |
| Job Function | |
| Telephone | Fax |
| Email Address | |
| Organization | |
| Address | |
| | |
| City | State/Zip |
| Web Site Address | |
| Administrative Assistant | |
| Telephone | |

### Additional Contacts

| Name | Function | Telephone | Fax |
|---|---|---|---|
| | | | |
| | | | |
| | | | |
| | | | |

### Contact History

| Contact | Results | Contact | Results |
|---|---|---|---|
| Date | | Date | |
| Contact | Results | Contact | Results |
| Date | | Date | |
| Contact | Results | Contact | Results |
| Date | | Date | |

**Follow-Up Activities**

| Activity | Results | Contact | Results |
|---|---|---|---|
| Responsibility | | Date | |
| Activity | Results | Contact | Results |
| Responsibility | | Date | |
| Activity | Results | Contact | Results |
| Responsibility | | Date | |

Additional Notes

_____

_____

_____

_____

_____

_____

_____

_____

_____

_____

_____

_____

_____

_____

_____

_____

_____

_____

**EXHIBIT 7.2**

## Letter to Foundations

**Letterhead**

Date

Contact Person
Title
Foundation (full name)
Address Line 1
Address Line 2
City, State, Zip

Dear (Mr/Mrs/Dr Name):

**Subject: Request for Information**

Please send information about your foundation, including the documents and publications listed below, if available. Enclosed is a self-addressed, stamped envelope in which to send the information.

- Annual report
- Guidelines for proposals
- Newsletter
- Information about past awards and awardees
- Areas of special interest and support

Thank you very much for your assistance.

Sincerely,

Your Name
Your Title

Enclosure: Self-addressed Stamped Return Envelope

The problem with all those, of course, is that it is hard to cross-reference the information so that each time there is a fundable project the right information can be located quickly and easily.

Creating an electronic database to keep your foundation information current is a good solution. If you want to create your own, there are a number of good database programs on the market.

1. Apple Macintosh Platform
   - FoxBASE
   - 4th Dimension
   - FileMaker Pro

2. MS-DOS Platform
   - dBase IV
   - Alpha 4
   - Paradox

Following is a list of some of the information on targeted foundations that should be kept in a database.

- Foundation name, address, telephone number
- Contact person, title
- Special areas of interest of the foundation
- Your matching project title(s) along with one or two sentences describing the project(s)
- Running history of contact with the foundation. Include the type of contact made (letter, phone call, visit) and dates, as well as a brief note concerning the result from each contact.
- List of information on hand on the foundation (newsletter, annual report, proposal guidelines, etc.)
- Record of the last date on which the file was updated.

If the research is tracked using hard copy, use the Foundation Contact Form as the cover sheet in your file. However you choose to organize your grantseeking efforts, think it through before you start. If you do not, you will wind up with stacks and stacks of paper and a lot of frustration!

### Step Six: Analyze Information and Narrow Choices  0702.DOC

Once your organization has received several packets of information from foundations, begin evaluating which ones are best bets for funding the project. You will want to look at such things as proximity, whether it has a past history of funding your type of program, range of awards, and whether the foundation's objectives match those of your project. Read every word of every document provided by the foundation. Every foundation has its own personality. Writing a proposal to a foundation is like writing a good letter—it is personal. Mom does not appreciate it if you send a form letter you could write to just anyone. Neither does a foundation. Use the form in Exhibit 7.3 to determine which foundation(s) fit best with your organization and project.

### Step Seven: Do More Research  0703.DOC

#### Past Awardees

Who are past awardees of grants from this organization? More to the point, why does your organization need to know? Foundations may indicate that they fund "health programs," and that they "fund programs in Northern Texas." This is good news if your organization is a health-oriented organization in Northern Texas. The foundation literature may look inviting, with a good match in problem interest and mission. Why should you go one more step? In the hypothetical case, we did take a further step and found that the only problem is that only one organization had ever been funded, "The Northern Texas Longhorn Health Crisis Clinic." If you are not with the Northern Texas Longhorn Health Crisis Clinic, what chance do you have for funding? Not much.

If you had skipped the last step, a lot of time and effort might have been wasted not to mention emotional energy, applying to a foundation that was never a possibility. Many people make this mistake. They find a directory of funders, get a list of names and addresses, and write proposals to each. Of course, they have no idea what kind of proposal is accepted by the funder, so there is one deadly strike against them. Even if they have gotten lucky and the funder has no particular required format, they still have no idea whether the foundation would ever entertain the idea of funding their project. These people frequently get turned down. It is very discouraging and gives an entirely false impression of grants acquisition.

Back to the main point: How do you find out about past awardees? The literature sent by the foundation may contain this information. Most annual reports list awardees. The contact person may tell you who some of the past awardees are over the telephone. There is a document to get, if all else fails—the Public Form (PF) 990.

The tax return of 501(c)(3) organizations are public, thus their Internal Revenue Service (IRS) tax returns have the nomenclature of PF 990. In other words, a PF 990 is the tax return filed with the IRS by a not-for-

# EXHIBIT 7.3

## Step Six—Analyze Material and Narrow Choices

Use the form below to help you determine which foundation(s) fit best with your organization and project. Check all boxes that apply or enter number where indicated.

| Foundation name | Is located within my state & funds programs in my area | Has a National funding range and funds programs in my state | Is located within 50 miles and funds programs in my area | Has past history of funding my type of organization | Degree to which stated objectives match objectives of my project (1–10 with 10 being best match) | Foundation award range matches desired funding for project | My project or organization meets "special credit" qualifications for this foundation | I have access to all information required by the foundation |
|---|---|---|---|---|---|---|---|---|
| Example XYZ Fdn | Yes | Yes | Yes | Yes | 7 | Yes | No | Yes |
| ABC Fdn | No | Yes | No | Yes | 4 | Yes | Yes | Need 501(c)3 |
|  |  |  |  |  |  |  |  |  |
|  |  |  |  |  |  |  |  |  |
|  |  |  |  |  |  |  |  |  |
|  |  |  |  |  |  |  |  |  |
|  |  |  |  |  |  |  |  |  |

profit organization. Grantmaking foundations are not-for-profit entities, so they all file a PF 990 yearly. One of the required items in each PF 990 is an identification of each organization or individual awarded a grant and the amount of the grant. At times, the grantor will include a short phrase explaining the purpose of the grant. This is not required by the IRS, so it cannot be counted on.

To fulfill the requirement that these forms be available to the public, most states' Secretary of State's offices keep copies of these forms filed and accessible to the public. They are also available at the regional IRS offices. However, the easiest way to obtain a copy is through the Foundation Center. Visit or call your local library that houses a Foundation Center Cooperating Collection. Request a copy of the PF 990 for the foundation(s) of your choice. The Foundation Center sends a microfiche copy to your local library, and your library creates a paper copy from the microfiche, charging you for the service, usually around 25 cents per page. A small foundation's PF 990 may run to as few as five pages, while the return for a very large foundation like the Ford Foundation may be 100 pages or longer.

## Champions

Who are the founder(s), board member(s), and trustees of the foundation? Many times, an organization is surprised to discover they have a connection to a local foundation. When that happens, and *if* you have a fundable project, the insider you know may become your champion and help shepherd your proposal within the foundation. Ask yourself a few questions. Record your answers on your Foundation Contact Form in the space provided.

- Do you, your colleagues, or anyone in your organization know any of the people listed? (If so, you may be able to foster a champion from within the foundation.)
- Search industry directories, located at your public library, for this information. *The Guide to U.S. Foundations: Their Trustees, Officers, and Donors* (published by The Foundation Center); and *The Foundation Directory* contain this information.

## Secondary Research

Using public library resources and other on-line resources, search for recent articles about your targeted foundation and its efforts. Search databases of newspapers, professional journals, and magazines. There may not be any articles, but if there are any, they can provide valuable information to help you focus the proposal.

Most national foundations and many local ones now have Internet web pages with information about the foundation's mission, application guidelines, programs sponsored, deadlines, and email addresses to ask questions.

### Step Eight: After Receiving the Proposal Guidelines or Request for Proposal, Make Three Outlines

As discussed in the section on researching federal sources, you will need to make three outlines, one each on proposal content, publishing requirements, and hot buttons. Because of the importance of making the outlines, a whole section is devoted to the issue of analyzing the funder's guidelines or request for proposal (RFP). Part III covers the entire analysis process, including how to make the three outlines. If the funder does not provide guidelines, then develop a proposal based on the information about proposal components and content provided in this book in Part IV.

## Now You Are Ready To . . .

You have completed your research on the targeted foundation. At this point, you should know for sure whether the program is a fit with your project. If so, you are ready for the next steps of the grants process. If not, then go back to Step One, Researching Foundation Funding Sources, and start over with another program; or move on to corporate funders and use the steps we have outlined to find the match.

# Chapter 8

# Researching Corporate Funding Sources

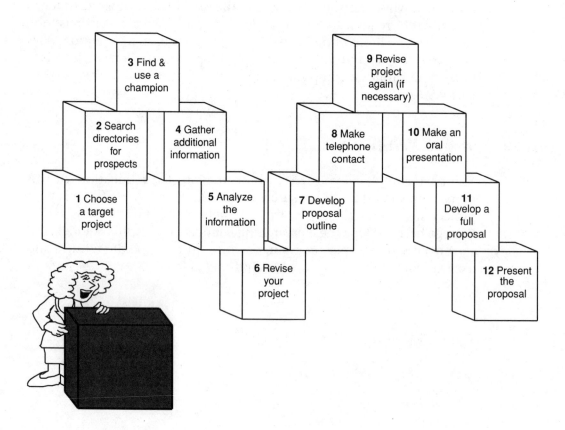

## Introduction

Corporations may sponsor a foundation and also may have a formal or informal giving program. Acquiring funds from a corporate giving program requires a somewhat different approach than that for a foundation or federal source. Approaching a corporation is much more personalized and direct than approaching most other sources. Giving by a company is limited to three circumstances: (1) companies with a major main office or facility located in your community, (2) companies with branch facilities in your community, and (3) companies that have a history of giving within your state or location regardless of whether there is a local facility in your community.

Of all the sources, corporations are most likely to give only to communities in which there is a corporate presence. Corporations want to benefit the communities of which they are a part. They want to provide support and assistance to their employees and their employees' families. A number of corporations publish brochures on giving programs in which you are told you have to have a company employee "sign off" on your application or proposal for it to be reviewed.

For successful corporate funding, it is very important to find and use a champion. A champion should be very informed about your project and what you are trying to accomplish, as well as the benefit of the project to the community and its residents. Champions are goodwill ambassadors for your project with the corporation you are approaching. Most often, the champion will be employed in the corporation, but sometimes he or she will just have a key contact or two.

Corporations are businesses and therefore require a highly business-like approach. Do not go to a company asking for a handout. It will rarely work. You must demonstrate a benefit to the company and/or its employees from supporting your project. Your proposal is like a business plan for your project. Corporate managers understand projects that are well developed and have a plan of action with expected results. Following our project development method and proposal writing process will position you quite well with a potential corporate funder.

Also, companies want to know specifically what you expect of them, early on in the process. It is therefore very important to have thoroughly thought out your project before approaching a corporation.

## RESEARCH STEPS FOR CORPORATE GRANTS—AN EXERCISE

0801.DOC–0806.DOC

### *Step One: Choose a Target Project*

As always, start the research process with a project. Though this is the third time we'll say this, it's so important, we'll repeat it again. To have a successful grants effort, projects should be developed continually, as problems are identified. Project profile sheets should be completed on each project, as per Exhibit 4.2.

### *Step Two: Search Industry Directories for Prospects*  0801.DOC

Your local library and/or university library will have some or all of the following directories that provide information on companies in your area. Ask the reference librarian to point you in the right direction.

- State business or manufacturing directory
- Dun & Bradstreet business and industry directories
- Ward's business directories
- Who's Who
- Dialog Information Service databases (expensive but effective)

Based on the profiles in the directory(ies), make a list of the corporations closest in proximity to your organization and/or those whose employees most use your services. In addition, note whether the corporate site is a home office, plant, branch office, district office, distribution facility, and so forth. Use the form provided on the disk to record your notes.

Review the information you recorded. What 5 to 10 corporations appear to be the best bets for funding your project? List them in the space provided on the Corporate Contact Sheet along with the contact, phone, and address.

### *Step Three: Find and Use a Champion*  0801.DOC

#### *Poll Your Staff Members*

Ask your staff members if any of them know anyone who works for the corporations you have targeted. Use the corporate contact sheet in Exhibit 8.1 and on the disk to record the name of the staff member, their

EXHIBIT **8.1**

## Step Three—Find and Use a Champion

Complete the following information on each of the corporations listed on the previous pages.

Corporation _____

Address _____

_____

Contact _____ Phone _____

- The following staff members know a contact person within the corporation.

| Staff Member | Corporate Contact | Job Title/Function |
|---|---|---|
|  |  |  |
|  |  |  |
|  |  |  |
|  |  |  |
|  |  |  |
|  |  |  |
|  |  |  |
|  |  |  |
|  |  |  |
|  |  |  |

contact, and the job title or function that contact holds in the corporation.

*Check with Board Members and Advisors*

Board members and members of advisory committees and councils are the second group to check with in your search for a champion. Again, use the corporate contact sheet to record the results of your research.

## Do Not Forget Community Supporters

Every established community organization has supporters. These are people who do not work for the organization and who may not currently serve on its boards, but who, for one reason or another, can be counted on for support. Sometimes these people are the very best bets for turning up corporate champions.

## Plan of Action

Once you have discovered a champion, then you need a plan of action to enlist his or her aid in championing the project to the corporation. Following are some questions to ask or information to determine. Write down your answers. It is very important that you have a professional plan in place before you approach your champion about helping you. You will have little luck if you appear indecisive and disorganized.

- What information about the project will be presented at the time of the initial contact?
- Who is responsible for gathering information for the initial meeting with the champion(s) and what is the deadline for publishing the information?
- Specifically what do we want the corporation to do for us?
- What do we want the potential champion to do for us?
- Who will make the initial contact with the champion(s) and when?

### Step Four: Gather Additional Information

The next step is to gather as much information concerning the company as possible. This information will help you plan your strategy to sell the company on supporting your project. The information gives you clues as to what is important to the company and what hot buttons to push in attaining support.

Most information can be acquired through the company public relations (public affairs, community relations), or marketing departments. *Important Note:* Some companies will have extensive information available, and some will have almost none. Some companies may consider some of the information confidential (such as the organization chart).

Either by letter, through your champion, or by telephone, ask the company for the following information:

- Annual report
- Newsletter

- Public relations or marketing pieces
- Organization chart
- Website address

Be careful to organize all the information you have gathered on each of the companies. In a grants effort, getting enough information to ensure success is key, but the paper can overwhelm you if you have not planned a way to organize and store it.

### Step Five: Analyze the Information  0802.DOC

Review the information you have gathered on each corporation and choose the one or two that are the best bets to support your project. It is very important to consider the influence of the corporate champion(s) you have identified for each corporation.

To help make a good choice, answer the following questions on each of the targeted corporations. It is sometimes a good idea to involve your champion in the planning at this stage. Sometimes he or she has inside information that can be helpful.

- What about the project might interest the company?
- Why should the company want to support the project?
- What are the benefits to the company in supporting the project?
- What evidence will you be able to show that the company's support and investment were worthwhile (accomplished the desired results)?

### Step Six: Revise the Project  0803.DOC

Review all the information you have gathered so far. Are there things you should change about your project to ensure a better fit with the funder?

Make a list of the things about your project you need to change/add/delete to make the project fit the funder's requirements and hot buttons. Rewrite your project description to reflect those changes.

### Step Seven: Develop a Proposal Outline  0804.DOC

In the case of a nonspecific corporate funding program, it is unlikely that there will be guidelines for preparing a proposal. You need a better idea, however, about what you are looking for before you talk to the potential funder. The best way of organizing and fleshing out your project idea is to outline it, as seen in Exhibit 8.2. Project outlining is covered in detail in Part III. Please refer to Chapter 10 for guidance.

Once you have a good project outline, consult your champion and discuss the project so that he or she is fully informed and can help you with your approach to the corporation.

### Step Eight: Make Telephone Contact  0805.DOC

The corporate contact person should be informed that you would like to set up a phone appointment to briefly discuss your project and set up a meeting. Use your champion to clear the way for your telephone call to the corporate contact person. A Conversation Guide is provided on the disk to help you prepare for this telephone call. As previously discussed, prepare thoroughly for this call. It must be brief and to the point. Do not waste the valuable time of the corporate contact person with unimportant information. This is not your only conversation; it is just an introduction to your project. Again, make your statements and then listen. The contact person may give you valuable information that will help you position your project.

### Step Nine: Revise the Project Again  0806.DOC

If your telephone conversation with the contact person warrants it, rewrite your draft project description to incorporate changes insuring a better fit with the funder.

### Step Ten: Make an Oral Presentation

As said before, working with a corporation is a highly personal, direct situation. Do not develop a full-blown proposal yet, because you want the benefit of a discussion with the corporate contact person to gain further valuable positioning information prior to putting details on paper. Prepare for the presentation by

- Preparing a one-page summary of your project, including a specific description of the support you desire from the company along with dollar figures, if appropriate. A suggested format and content topics are included below.

- Preparing your champion to accompany you and support your project. Be sure the champion fully understands the project and the support needed from the company.

## Exhibit 8.2

## Step Seven—Develop a Proposal Outline

Using the model in Chapter 8, outline your project from the first step to the last. The Roman numerals represent the major steps to take to set up, implement, and evaluate your project. The capital letters under each Roman numeral are the steps to accomplish the activities indicated by the statements beside the Roman numerals. Include dollar figures and resources needed.

| Outline | Resources Needed | Cost |
|---|---|---|
| I. Determine the content of the special curriculum | *The dollar figure to the right equals the total of the costs of all steps under this Roman numeral | *$2,859 |
| A. Hold facilitated planning session with instructional specialists | Instructional consultant<br>Meeting room<br>Printing for agendas, etc.<br>Postage<br>Note pads, pencils, name tags<br>Travel expenses for state personnel | $2,000<br>50<br>20<br>5<br>50<br>560 |
| B. Create report | Data entry<br>Paper<br>Binders<br>Copying | $64<br>22<br>50<br>38 |

- "Training" another person to act as presenter as you answer technical questions, if you are technically versed in the project details, but are not a polished spokesperson.
- Keeping the presentation to less than 15 minutes. Be brief and concise. Absolutely do not expand your presentation beyond the time limit.

*Project Summary—Content and Format*

1. About your organization (two or three pertinent facts)—1 or 2 minutes

   *Example*: We serve 2,300 people, 40 percent of which are classified as disadvantaged, and 30 percent of which either work in your company, or who have family working in your company.

**2.** About the problem—1 or 2 minutes

*Example*: The people we serve remain at low income levels because their basic skills are so poor that they cannot train for and acquire skilled jobs. According to Mr. James, your company has difficulty training your people because of their poor reading and math skills.

**3.** About the solution (your project)—5 minutes

*Example*: Our project attempts to raise the level of basic skills, first with a test group of 25 individuals, and then, after appropriate revision, the project will be extended to others in the community, including, if you agree, your employees. Here is how the project works. . . .

**4.** About the need for support from the company—2 minutes

*Example*: We can fund XYZ parts of the project which include staff, facilities, and supplies. We need $4,326 for equipment including ABC and CDE. This equipment will be used to FGH.

**5.** Discussion (leave time here for questions and answers)—time frame depends on the contact person

**6.** Call to action (what are the next steps?)—3–5 minutes

*Example*: We would like for you and any other people in your company who might be interested to tour our facility and see firsthand what we are trying to do. Then, when all the details of the project are ironed out, we would like to present you with a full, written proposal. We should have that completed week after next. When might you be able to come visit us? We will be glad to treat you to lunch.

### Step Eleven: Develop a Full Proposal

Develop a concise but detailed proposal. There probably will not be proposal guidelines from the potential funder, so, in this case, proceed with project development and proposal writing according to the guidance provided in Parts III and IV of this book.

*Important Note*: A proposal to a company to obtain its support, whether financial or otherwise, combines business planning, marketing, and public relations. In developing the proposal, review what you know about the company and the contact person with whom you are working. Be sure to address the issues that are important to the company, such as how the project will help the community in which the company's employees work.

### Step Twelve: Present the Proposal

Hand deliver a professionally "packaged" proposal within 10 days after your meeting. Your proposal is a professional business proposal. Be careful to package your proposal in a binder that is commonly used in business and industry circles. A report binder, one that a student might use, is not appropriate. A local quick-print firm can bind the proposal for you inexpensively.

If you cannot hand deliver the proposal, use a courier or express mailing service so that you have a receipt to indicate that the proposal was delivered appropriately.

# Chapter 9

# Researching State and Local Funding Sources

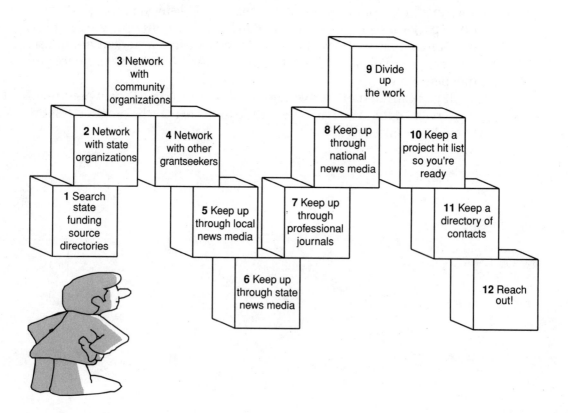

3 Network with community organizations

2 Network with state organizations

4 Network with other grantseekers

1 Search state funding source directories

5 Keep up through local news media

6 Keep up through state news media

7 Keep up through professional journals

8 Keep up through national news media

9 Divide up the work

10 Keep a project hit list so you're ready

11 Keep a directory of contacts

12 Reach out!

# Introduction

Finding state and local funding sources is more difficult than finding national, foundation, and federal sources. Why? State and local programs change more frequently and are not normally effectively publicized within a state or locality.

State and local sources are likely to be publicized down through the bureaucratic chain of command. Typically, this causes problems for grantseekers because they find out about the source too close to the deadline for submission of a proposal.

In addition, state and local programs are frequently highly political in nature, so finding out about state and local funding availability becomes a matter of who you know and who you have talked to recently.

So what are the keys to getting in on state and local funding? Networking and keeping current are the keys to success with state and local sources.

Following are ways to network and stay current.

# Search State Directories of Funding Sources

Since many organizations in each state regularly seek grant funding, almost all states have locally prepared information about some state funding sources. These directories are usually found in the public library, university library, or in the private libraries of other grantseekers (e.g., the United Way office).

# Network with State Organizations

Becoming involved with others who seek grants is an invaluable activity. In many cases, the only way to find out about state and local funding possibilities in through word of mouth avenues. Following are some types of organizations to consider.

### State Departments of Agencies

Often, a state department of an agency has a newsletter or other mechanism to let local agencies know about funding opportunities. It is possible that all you need to do is get on the right mailing list. If you cannot get on the mailing list, find out who is on the list and ask that person if you can have a copy of the document when it is received.

Much of the funding for which your projects may be eligible may come from other departments in the state. If your project relates to development of job skills, then the Department of Labor might be a likely funder. If your project relates to development of environmental or conservation awareness, the Wildlife Department or Environmental Protection Agency might be a resource. If your project has to do with families, the Department of Education or the Department of Health and Human Services (Department of Social Services) may be your best bet.

### Governor's Office

In many states, the governor's office produces newsletters and bulletins about projects in which the state is interested. In addition, each governor has special causes for which funding is allocated. Your project may fit nicely with one of these areas of special interest.

### Development Boards, Special Councils, Consortiums, or Initiatives

At both the state and local levels, there are numerous special groups with a mission to initiate activities to solve a variety of problems. Many of these groups either have funding to let or know about funding within their particular area of interest. If your project fits within the scope of one of these special groups, contact with the group may turn up a great deal of support for your project.

### Professional Associations

Professional associations usually are grantseekers themselves. Their directors are usually involved in networks of other grants persons. In addition, many associations offer special services related to grantseeking—newsletters, technical assistance, and/or training.

## Network with Community Organizations

Many community organizations such as Shriners, Civitan, business councils, and others sponsor a variety of projects in your community. Frequently, it takes only some direct contact, perhaps a presentation at a meeting, and some elbow grease to gain local support to initiate your project.

## Network with Other Grantseekers

There are many pockets of grantseekers in a given community. By and large, these people are very happy to help less experienced grantseekers connect with resources. Sometimes, a fellow grantseeker can provide valuable insight into the "psychology" of grantseeking or of approaching a particular source. It is particularly valuable to make contact with grantseekers who are *not* in organizations that could compete with yours for funding. The following are some places to look:

- Universities and colleges
- Technical or vocational schools and colleges
- Local development boards and councils
- Nonprofit organizations

## Keep Up

Funding follows problems. There was a time when there was no funding related to drug abuse problems. There was a time when there was no funding to attack problems related to teen pregnancy. Grantseekers who kept up and who had good ideas about how to solve a growing drug problem probably got in on the first funding let to solve the drug problems. These wise grantseekers knew that the more publicity appearing in public media about a problem, the more likely that money would follow. Those submitting good proposals early on, when funding has just been let, have a good chance at that funding because there is much less competition.

It would be a good idea to regularly read the following:

- National newspapers and magazines (especially if your project is a potential model program)
- State newspapers
- Local newspapers
- Professional journals

## State and Local Funding Sources  0901.DOC

Make your own "directory" of contacts and resources you and your colleagues can use to help you acquire state and local funding. Use the worksheet provided on the disk to record the information.

## Research Plan  0501.DOC

Whether you are looking for federal, foundation, corporate, or state or local funding, you need a plan for your research. The plan is needed for many reasons, but chief is to keep you on track and from wasting time. Also, a good plan can be used as a tool to help you delegate some of the responsibility. Included with this book is a Research Plan Template to help you organize your funder research efforts.

Here are some tips and guidelines to help you develop your plan. Design a plan to capture and catalog the information so that research does not have to be done over and over again.

Carefully think through a plan to organize and store the information you acquire from your research efforts. Except for updating information about sources, the basic information, once gathered, can save valuable time on the next proposal. Following are some suggestions and questions to ponder.

- What people within your extended organization will want to be involved in the grants effort? Grants acquisition should be a team effort. What team members will need the information gathered through your research?

- What resources can you acquire that will save time running back and forth to the public library. Consider asking community supporters to donate references.

- If you choose to set up computer databases to store information you receive about funding sources, consider setting up special files in a centralized location so others seeking grants will not have to redo research that has already been done.

- You will certainly need to set up files to maintain hard copy. Consider centralizing those files as well.

- If there are a large number of people in your organization seeking grants, or if grantseekers are spread out among several locations, consider setting up a communications mechanism via electronic mail or memo to regularly inform people about new information as it comes in.

- It is a good idea to designate a person to specialize in a given type of source research (such as for foundation or federal sources). Each type of source has its own "personality" and system of research. Once someone is familiar with the peculiarities of a given source, the research goes much faster.

- Consider enlisting the aid of persons outside your organization to assist with the research efforts: retired business persons, retired instructional personnel, parents of students, and so forth.

- Partner with other grantseeking organizations to spread out the research duties.

- Enlist the aid of local public library personnel. They can be valuable resources to help you find the best way to organize your research information.
- Use searchable databases (when cost effective) to aid in your efforts. Determine what information is best acquired through these services.

# Developing the Final Project

# Chapter 10

# Analyzing the Grantmaker's Guidelines or Request for Proposal

## *Introduction*

All the research with potential federal, foundation, and corporate funders has been to gain information to determine the best way to approach the funding issue. Just as a person would think of signing loan papers, entering into an agreement for employment, or committing to a lease without first thoroughly researching the terms of the agreements, the veracity of the other party, and our ability to fulfill the contract, we should not approach the grantmaker recklessly. The reason is that obtaining a grant is signing a contract. You contract with the grantmaker to do what you said you would do in your proposal in return for the money with which to do it. Analyzing the potential funder's proposal guidelines or request for proposal (RFP) outlines the required terms of the grant contract. More than that, it explains exactly how to write the proposal—the contract document—to be eligible for the funds.

According to inside sources, an average of 60 percent of the proposals received by funders are eliminated on first review because the preparer submitting the proposal did not follow directions or had not made a project match. The requirements were not met or the questions in the RFP were not answered.

It is very important, then, to understand exactly what the funder expects in a proposal and with regard to the project. This section of the book will provide concrete guidance to help ensure that the proposal makes it beyond that first review. Remember, this book was prepared to help your proposals all place in the top 10 percent of those received by funders.

Every grantseeker eventually understands that analyzing the RFP is a necessity. What does it mean to analyze an RFP? It means determining what belongs in the proposal. Learning the rules. Learning how to organize the proposal. Learning what questions to answer. The information needed to create a winning proposal fits comfortably into four topics: Hot Buttons, Proposal Content, Publishing Requirements, and Questions. In this section, each of these four topics will be explained. Following the explanations in Appendix 10.A, an entire RFP is reproduced. Following the RFP, a possible analysis of this RFP is reproduced.

## Potential Funder's Guidelines or Request for Proposal

Look back in Part II of this book for step-by-step processes for getting information about what a potential funder wants to know about the project and how to present a proposal. Every funder is different—not just every type of funder, but every funder within the type. Federal funders are different from foundation funders, who are different from corporate funders. Within the category of federal funders, each program is different and has different requirements. There may be similarities, but the processes and proposal requirements are different.

## Contacting the Grantmaker

Many foundations indicate the first approach is by letter. Does this mean you do not write a proposal? No, the "letter proposal" is perhaps the hardest one to write. It is the same as having to present the whole project so anyone on the street can understand it, but with a 200-word limit.

During our workshops, one of the biggest complaints is how difficult it is to create a project synopsis and stay within the space limitations. We are asked things like, "What if I extend the margins out just a quarter of an inch?" or "What if I reduce the font size just one point?" Of course, they are told absolutely not to cheat. After all, what impression are you giving the reader—that you are willing to cheat rather than attend to the letter and intent of the "law," the rules set forth by the funder? Admittedly, the less space you have, the more difficult it is to fully describe a project, and thus the letter proposal requires extreme organization and conciseness, as well as ultimate restraint. Taking off on tangents is not tolerated. Most of the topics in a full-blown proposal, must be included, but with a limit of only a sentence or two each in which to tell your story.

At the opposite end of the spectrum from the "letter proposal" is the no-limit, "we want every tiny little detail explained several different ways" proposal. We call this one the kitchen sink proposal. Kitchen sink proposals are the dinosaurs of the grant world. In the past, it seemed that proposals were judged more by the pound than by content. As more and more people are applying for grant funding, virtually burying some grantmakers in paper, grantmakers are becoming wiser about sparing themselves the unnecessary time and effort of wading through stacks of superfluous information. They are becoming increasingly specific about what they want to see in a proposal. The trend is toward strict page limits and well-thought-out guidelines.

As with anything else, most grant proposals fall somewhere in the middle of the two extremes. Whatever type of proposal is required, it is necessary to have a fully developed project before you ever begin writing. This cannot be stressed enough. The major mistake people make is in picking up a set of guidelines and, armed with just a project idea, starting to write. Writing the proposal is just 10 percent to 15 percent of the task at hand. Planning the project is where the successful grantseekers concentrate their efforts.

This section will discuss how to analyze the funder's guidelines or RFP to ensure that your proposal is "responsive," meaning that it meets all the proposal requirements set forth by the funder. In addition, this section will help to ensure that you have responded appropriately to all questions about your project. A thorough analysis of the funder's requirements provides a last check and balance for your project to be sure it's a match with the funder.

## Make a Hot Buttons Outline

What are sales hot buttons? This question directly relates to the tone and stance of a proposal. A proposal is a marketing piece. It is a persuasive narrative. Through or with the proposal, you are selling the funder on the idea that your project is the best one in which to invest. You need to communicate your confidence and pride in your project in a professionally persuasive manner.

Too often, proposals read like college term papers, with no passion or conviction. The project may be a very good one, but its innovation and excellence are hidden in a forest of stiff rhetoric and jargon.

Another common problem with some proposals is that they are maudlin. Remember, grant funders are looking to make a good investment in a workable, beneficial project. They have already identified one or more problems they believe should be solved. They are not going to award competitive project grant money based on who has the worst sob story. They do care, but they are practical enough to look carefully at the project and its likelihood for success. Certainly, you will cover the problem and the need for the project, but with a focus on the project results intended and with a decidedly professional tone.

So, now that we know what not to do, what *do* we do? We carefully read all the material available from the funder, especially that which is included in the RFP, and we identify the issues that are of key importance. These issues—hot buttons—are sales points. When the project addresses one of those issues, clearly point it out—push those hot buttons. If you think about it, that is exactly what good marketers do. They find out what outcomes are important to their target market and they describe how their product addresses those outcomes. Every issue that is important to the funder that your project also matches gives you an increasing edge over projects that do not as directly address key points.

## Hot Button—Definition and Examples

A hot button is something, anything, that the grantor cares enough about to mention with passion in the RFP. *Passion,* in this case, means finding such phrases as the following:

- "Some of the most exciting possibilities . . ."
- "Failure to . . . put their future . . . at risk . . ."
- "Potential for creative synergy . . ."
- "These powerful learning tools . . ."
- "Opportunity to become personally engaged . . ."
- "Children stand a greater chance of success . . ."

When encountering phrases such as these, ask this question: "What is the cause of this passion?" Another method to determine the key hot button is to construct a question around the topic. First, use a question-making phrase such as "what is/are" or "why do/does." Next, follow the question-making phrase with the passionate phrase. Sometimes it works better to follow the passionate phrase with the question-making phrase "to what." This simple process constructs questions like this:

- What are some of the most exciting possibilities?
- Why does failure to . . . put their future . . . at risk?
- What is potential for creative synergy?
- What are these powerful learning tools?
- What is the opportunity to become personally engaged?
- Why do children stand a greater chance of success?

When the question has been carefully, thoughtfully, and honestly answered, a hot button is defined. When all the hot buttons are listed, there will be a great deal of repetition. This is to be expected. In fact, it is one of the purposes of uncovering all the hot buttons. Often, when a hot button is repeated, new information or facts can be added to the basic or overall hot button topic.

The way to create a good list of hot buttons is to first list every hot button you find, regardless of repetitions. Once you have worked your way from the first page of the RFP to the last and have listed all hot buttons, go back and collect all similar hot buttons together. What looks like a hundred or more hot buttons usually will turn out to be 10 to 20. Do this once, and once it is done, it is an invaluable resource.

## Project Related Hot Buttons

Another type of hot button is a fact or an instruction. That is, a hot button may be giving definite instruction about an aspect of the project or the proposal. Also, a hot button may be establishing boundaries of time or money. The following are a few typical facts that belong in this section of an RFP analysis:

- Length of the project; usually in years, sometimes in months
- Size of budget; usually a minimum and maximum are given
- Definition of eligible legal applicant or fiscal agent
- Grantor contact person name and telephone number, and perhaps email address

Exhibit 10.1 is an example of a quotation from an RFP and the resulting hot buttons outline.

EXHIBIT **10.1**

## RFP Quotation, Hot Buttons Outline

### Example

". . . encourages the participation of private sector organizations and technical personnel . . . carefully developed partnerships can make industrial technical knowledge and experience available for the enhancement of science education . . . the primary focus must be the blending of the scientific, technical, organizational, and management skills of the noneducation world with the knowledge and pedagogical expertise of educators . . . types of special interest are: developing science or mathematics 'literacy' courses . . . organizations serving rural populations will receive priority . . ."

### Outline of Sales Points

I. Private sector participation
   A. Industry partnerships focused on technical knowledge as applied to science education
   B. Blend scientific, technical, organizational, and management skills from industry
   C. Use knowledge and pedagogical expertise of educators
II. Literacy courses
III. Rural service population

## MAKE A PROPOSAL CONTENT OUTLINE—AN EXERCISE

In the average grantmaker's proposal guidelines or RFP, direct requests for information about your project will be intertwined with other information. Some content requirements will be very clear and some will be more vague. Reading and rereading are necessary to ensure that you have found every point.

Proposal content means the items to be included in the proposal, their names, their order, and what should be included in each item. Note that what an item, section, part, or subdivision is called by the grantor is what we will call it. For example, you may be in the habit of including a time line in your proposals. But what if a grantor asks for a "calendar of events" in the RFP you are analyzing? Then, we label what we have in the past called a time line a calendar of events. You may be familiar with organizing a project with an overall mission and goals and objectives as steps to accomplish the mission. But what if the grantor asks for the goal of the project and several activities leading to the accomplishment of the project goal? Then, what we called a mission before now becomes the goal, and what we called goals before now are labeled activities. In short, we use the grantor's titles.

Use the grantor's order. We may be comfortable with first telling about our need or problem, then giving our project plan in outline or summary form, then fully explaining our project. This makes sense to us. It is the way we do things. But what if the grantor asks for your goals and objectives first, then a project summary, then your statement of need, then your project plan narrative? Then, we follow the grantor's order. It does not have to make sense to us. Our task when responding to an RFP is to follow directions.

As stated earlier, throughout the RFP, the funder tells you what content must appear in the proposal. Since discussion of content appears in many sections of the RFP, it is absolutely necessary to make an outline to keep from missing any important points. The simplest way to ensure that nothing is missed is to comb each and every paragraph in an RFP, including forms, introductory material, tables, graphics, captions, lists—everything. Once all the content of a paragraph is transferred to one of the outlines—proposal content, hot buttons, publishing, and questions—then put a check mark by that paragraph. Never look at that paragraph again. Once every paragraph, graphic, caption, note, or list on a page has a check mark beside it, put a check in the upper right-hand corner of the page. Never look at that page again. Once every page of the RFP has a check mark on it, you are finished. This process will take three to four hours once you get the hang of it. At first, you may spend six to eight hours, but it will be time well spent. You will be, in effect, "studying" the RFP, and you will be putting it into a useful form, a form that you can directly use. Anyone who has paged back and forth through an RFP for days on end while creating a proposal will understand the value of creating these four outlines.

The content of your proposal must match exactly the content the funder requests. Exhibit 10.2 shows examples of direct quotations from funding guidelines and resulting content outlines.

## MAKE AN OUTLINE OF PUBLISHING REQUIREMENTS—AN EXERCISE

Throughout the RFP, the funder tells you what must appear in the proposal and how. Typically, discussion of publishing requirements appears in many sections of the RFP; therefore, making an outline essential. The publishing of your proposal must exactly match the funder's requirements, so it is important not to leave anything out. Following are some of the things that come under the topic of publishing requirements.

## Exhibit 10.2

### Funding Guidelines—Content Outline

**Example**

"List the project's needs, the basis for determining the local needs that the partnership will address should be described in detail.

Write goals. The goals should consist of a few broad statements appropriate to the needs addressed by the proposal. List a number of objectives that will lead to the achievement of each goal. Describe in detail the activities proposed to achieve each objective.

Indicate clearly the roles of the various members of the partnership. Give quantitative data appropriate to the project design, such as the number of participants expected in a workshop, the number and type of workshop materials to be prepared, or the number of participants to be placed into internships in industry."

**Content Outline**

   I. Project Need
      A. Local need
      B. Partnership addressing of need
  II. Goals and objectives
 III. Activities under each objective
 IV. Roles of partners
  V. Project design
      A. Number of participants
      B. Number of workshop materials prepared
      C. Type of workshop materials
      D. Number of participants to be placed in internships in industry

### *Page Limitations*

As mentioned previously, most funders are now limiting the length of proposals. Page limitations can be for the narrative portion of the proposal only or there can be separate page limitations for each section of the proposal from narrative to budget. Sometimes, there will be an overall page limitation.

It is important to point out that page limitations are absolute. Cheating is not allowed, and for good reason. If you will cheat on page limitations, what will you do if you get into a tough spot with your project? Funders frequently use page limits as the first "rite of passage," initially doing a page count on submitted proposals, throwing away all those exceeding the limits.

Okay, so if we cannot include all the information in the body of the proposal because of the limitations, then we will just put the leftovers in the appendix. Right? Wrong! The appendix is the first place most funders limit. Many tell you exactly what to put in the appendix and issue the warning, "Extraneous material will decrease your chances for success." It is a nice way of saying, "Do not use the appendix for a dumping ground." The appendix should contain only the material required, or if there are no requirements, only information that will significantly enhance the proposal but would interrupt the train of thought if put in the body of the document. Nothing should be put in the appendix that is not directly, and necessarily, referred to in the body of the proposal.

### Margins and Fonts

Any funder who has received a proposal typed in a tiny font (to get more words on a page?) subsequently specifies the font size requirement! Why someone would want to make reading the proposal hard on the reader is puzzling, but it happens. We have seen everything from elaborate script-like fonts to handwritten proposals, from small fonts to pages faded out from lack of ink in the printer. There was once a proposal almost entirely taken from faxed pages, most of which were nearly unreadable. Did any of these proposals win? The answer is a resounding "no!" They were not even reviewed.

Besides font size, many funders tell you what margin is required. Obviously, this is to prevent people from running the type right out to the edges of the pages in an attempt to get more words on a page.

### Paper, Binding, and Number of Copies

Most funders will state that the proposal is to be presented in black ink on plain white paper. Some people have submitted proposals on colored paper under the false assumption that this makes their proposals stand out from others. It may, but it leaves the wrong impression. It sends the signal to the funder that the one who submitted the proposal thinks the proposal process is a game in which some sort of trick is the winning strategy. This is not a lottery. It is a professional business exchange. As mundane as it may seem, a business format on white paper is the best bet.

Usually, funders ask that documents be delivered unbound. There are several reasons for this, most often so additional copies can be made easily. Frequently, different parts of the proposal will be reviewed by different people. The budget may go to a finance expert, and the narrative to a content expert.

Funders will frequently require more than one copy to be submitted. This is because several people may be reviewing the document. Be sure to send the number of copies requested.

### Page Numbering and Table of Contents

Many funders will specify page numbering and will discuss what must be included in a table of contents.

### Deadlines

Guidelines will tell you when to submit a proposal. If the funder says proposals must be received by a certain day and time, it is absolute, so it is very important not to miss this detail when reviewing the proposal guidelines.

Exhibit 10.3 is an example of a direct quotation from an RFP.

## MAKE A LIST OF QUESTIONS—AN EXERCISE

During the process of finding hot buttons, creating the proposal content outline, and picking out the publishing guidelines, you will come across things that you do not understand or cannot figure out. There is, of course, only one source that can answer your questions—the grantor. You have two choices. Each time you come across something baffling, get on the telephone to the contact person and get an answer. After about the fifth call, the grantor has developed a mental picture of you that you would not find complementary. The better choice is to collect all your questions, in writing, and make one telephone call, during which you get all the answers in one conversation.

When you come across something you do not understand or cannot figure out during the process of RFP analysis, write out the question in your list of questions. No question is too trivial. The only criteria for writing out a question is that there is something about which you are not clear. The first few times you go through this process, your list of questions may be huge. Do not despair. The list will become smaller and smaller as you gain experience.

Also, do not fear calling the contact person. Grantors want to answer your questions. Grantors need good projects, and they are more than willing to give you all the help they can. It is true that they are busy and do not want to be needlessly bothered. However, a 15-minute telephone call from a knowledgeable applicant who has obviously and carefully prepared for the call is welcomed by grantors.

## EXHIBIT 10.3

## RFP Quotation—Publishing Requirement Outline

### Example

"One copy of the cover sheet must be signed by the proposed project director and by an authorized institutional representative . . . Pagination should begin with 1 and the Table of Contents and continue in sequence to the end of the biographies . . . Describe the project in 200 words or less . . . While the number of pages for each item is not fixed, the total narrative must not exceed 15 unreduced single-spaced 8½" by 11" pages . . . Complete a separate budget sheet for each full year of the project . . . Mail 10 copies and the original to NSF, 1515 South Whatever Street, Washington, DC 22222."

### Outline of Publishing Requirements

I. Forms
    A. Cover sheet—one copy signed by project director and institutional rep
    B. Budget sheets—complete a separate one for each project year
II. Pagination
    A. Start with 1—include the Table of Contents in numbering
III. Page limitations
    A. Project description—200 words or less
    B. Project narrative—15 pages
IV. Formatting requirements
    A. Unreduced
    B. Single spaced
    C. 8½" by 11" pages
V. Mailing instructions
    A. 10 copies
    B. 1 original
    C. To XYZ, 1515 South Whatever Street, Washington, DC 22222.

## Appendix 10.A

## Case Study—Technology Innovation Challenge Grants: RFP and Model Outline

## Exhibit 10A.1

## Technology Innovation Challenge Grants

### Technology Innovation Challenge Grants

Applications Due: May 30, 1997

Office of Educational Research and Improvement

U.S. Department of Education
Phone: 202-208-3882
Fax: 202-208-4042
E-mail: ITO STAFF1@ed.gov

**U.S. DEPARTMENT OF EDUCATION HOME PAGE**
http://www.ed.gov/Technology

\* Technology Innovation Challenge Grants are the next generation of an initiative that began as the Challenge Grants for Technology in Education, and they are counterparts of the new Technology Literacy Challenge Fund.

### Table of Contents

### The Challenge

How can we use new technology and the information superhighway to improve education and increase economic competitiveness? Modern computers and telecommunication networks are powerful tools. But the hardware alone is not enough to improve learning. Sustained professional development for teachers and effective software, well integrated with the curriculum, are essential to help students meet high academic standards.

This is an ambitious challenge. We are experiencing a scientific and technological revolution of unprecedented proportions. Everywhere we look, technology is changing the way we work and live. Everywhere, that is, but in our classrooms. In the information age, we have industrial era schools. In classrooms that could be modern communication centers for learning, the basic media of instruction are blackboards and chalk.

Community leaders and educators are excited about the possibilities for transforming their classrooms into information age learning centers, but few school systems can afford the costs and risks associated with developing new, high quality applications of technology on their own. Similarly, few school systems working alone, have all the expertise and resources they need to integrate these learning innovations into the curriculum on a system-wide basis. Technology Innovation Challenge Grants provide seed money to form community partnerships that can bear these costs and marshal these resources. These consortia bring telecommunications, hardware and software expertise to schools in combination with the educational resources of universities, research institutes, libraries and museums.

As catalysts for change, Technology Innovation Challenge Grants support educators and parents, industry partners, community leaders and others who are collaboratively developing new applications of technology to transform their factory era schools into information age learning centers. Some of the most exciting possibilities might flow from a creative synthesis of ideas generated by teachers and students, who are working with software developers and cognitive researchers in consortia that include: telecommunication firms and hardware manufacturers, entertainment producers, and others who are stretching our thinking about how to create new learning communities.

Technology Innovation Challenge Grants have the potential to improve education by building on computer and telecommunication advances that create powerful new ways to discover knowledge and exchange information. We learn more when we are solving challenging problems in meaningful contexts. Our mastery of new knowledge becomes stronger when we actively collaborate with others to communicate our understanding of what we have learned. The extent of learning and the effectiveness of teaching need no longer be limited by the amount of time in the classroom or by the resources of a particular school. Teachers and students can tap vast electronic libraries and museums with a wealth of texts, video images, music, arts and languages. They can work with scientists and scholars around the globe who can help them use experimental research, primary historical documents, and authentic learning in real life settings to improve their understanding of physical phenomena and world events.

Technology Innovation Challenge Grant consortia need not be limited by geography. The information superhighway creates new possibilities for extending the time, the place, and the resources for learning. It can bring high quality education and training to every classroom, workplace, and home in the community at any time of day. The information superhighway can be used to create new learning communities linking schools, colleges, libraries, museums, and businesses across the country or around the world.

Technology Innovation Challenge Grant consortia are encouraged to act on their most ambitious visions for technology in education reform. But, we must not become a society in which students from low income communities, and other areas in need of technology, are left behind in the acquisition of knowledge and skills for responsible citizenship and productive work in the 21st century. Failure to include these communities will put their future, and the future of the country, at risk. In awarding Technology Innovation Challenge Grants, the U.S. Secretary of Education will evaluate

*(continued)*

## Exhibit **10A.1** *Continued*

the extent to which the proposed project is designed to serve areas with a high number or percentage of disadvantaged students or the greatest need for education technology.

### Who Can Apply for a Technology Innovation Challenge Grant?

Potential applicants should be aware that Technology Innovation Challenge Grants are highly competitive awards. In 1995 there were 530 applicants for 19 grants. In 1996 a total of 586 applicants competed for 24 grants. **At the time of this announcement it is estimated that twenty (20) new grants will be awarded by September 30, 1997.**

**Challenge Grants are five-year awards, and each applicant must propose five years of activity. Grants will range from $250,000 a year to $1,500,000 a year, with the average being $900,000 a year for five years. Applications that exceed $1,500,000 for any year of the five year project, and applications proposing less than five full years of work, will not be considered (these applications will be returned to the applicant without review).**

Each application must be submitted by a Local Education Agency (LEA) on behalf of a consortium of partners with appropriate resources to develop innovative applications of technology that will address specific learning needs identified in the application (a definition of LEA appears on p. 9). Each consortium must include at least one local educational agency with a high percentage or number of children living below the poverty line. Moreover, the U.S. Secretary of Education will evaluate the extent to which the assistance sought is designed to serve areas with a high number of percentage of disadvantaged students or the greatest need for access to educational technology. The consortium may also include other local education agencies and private schools, State Education Agencies and institutions of higher education, museums and libraries, hardware manufacturers, software designers, telecommunication firms, and other businesses or appropriate community organizations.

The consortium holds the potential for a creative synergy among its members. The partners should be carefully chosen for their potential to develop innovative applications of technology for improved learning. A consortium's efforts should be clearly designed to encourage ongoing involvement of educators, students, parents, business leaders, and others who are committed to school improvement and education reform. Specific objectives for active participation by each consortium member at each stage of development will contribute to success.

Technology Innovation Challenge Grants are five-year development and demonstration projects. Each consortium should have plans in place to begin start-up activities in year one, including initial trials of new learning content and sustained professional development for teachers (Technology Innovation Challenge Grants are not planning grants). Years two and three should be devoted to refinement and expansion of the new applications of technology. Years four and five should support systemwide adoptions that can become self sustaining after the fifth year.

The Technology Innovation Challenge Grant can not be the only source of support for a consortium's work. Under the selection criteria for this competition, applications will be evaluated on the extent to which members of the consortium make substantial commitments for the costs of equipment, technical support, network linkage, telecommunication services, and other resources.

Specific contributions of consortium members should be clearly identified and documented in the application. The projected contributions should be realistic and credible. The application should include convincing plans for long-term support of the innovation after the grant ends. Challenge Grant consortia are encouraged to demonstrate how other community partnerships can adapt and sustain these innovations in their schools on a cost-effective basis.

Funding provided by Technology Innovation Challenge Grants should augment the investment of consortium members by supporting the development of interactive learning content, continuous professional development for teachers, and instructional strategies that integrate new technologies into the curriculum. **Applications in which the primary purpose is to equip schools, build networks, or obtain operating funds for existing systems have not been successful in this competition in the past.**

Consortium commitments may be augmented by state or local bond issues and funding initiatives. They may include volunteer activities such as Tech Corps, and Net Days. Additional sources of support may include foundation grants, private corporate sponsorship, and other philanthropic contributions.

Technology Innovation Challenge Grant consortia may draw on a wide range of federal government sources for support. For example, with assistance from the U.S. Department of Education, communities across the country have developed district-wide and state-wide school reform plans to meet the National Education Goals, and these plans provide an ideal context for demonstrating the use of new technologies to improve learning. Other U.S. Department of Education programs may contribute to the success of a consortium's effort, including: Title I of the Improving America's Schools Act; the Eisenhower Professional Development Program; School-to-Work Opportunities; Star Schools; the Regional Technology for Education Consortia; the Regional Educational Laboratories, and the Technology Literacy Challenge Fund, which is the companion initiative of the Technology Innovation Challenge Grants.

Other federal agency programs also may complement or strengthen the work of a Technology Innovation Challenge Grant. The U.S. Department of Commerce helps communities to develop telecommunication infrastructure. The National Science Foundation supports the use of technology for improved mathematics and science education. The National Aeronautics and Space Administration funds initiatives to improve the use of space science data in the classroom. The U.S. Department of Housing and Urban Development supports networked neighborhoods and the "Campus of Learners" in public housing. The Department of Health and Human Services is interested in carefully conceived demonstrations of how new technologies can improve learning in Head Start and pre-school settings.

Funds from other federal sources, including those provided through the Technology Literacy Challenge Fund, may not be commingled with Technology Innovation Challenge Grant funds, or counted as costs supported by the LEA or other sources in the budget section of the application, however. The substantive contribution of each federal effort, and the cumulative impact of these activities, should be described in the Technology Innovation Challenge Grant application. But the budget for each federally funded effort or activity must be administered separately.

*(continued)*

**Exhibit 10A.1** *Continued*

### What Can You Do with a Technology Innovation Challenge Grant?

Challenge Grant consortia must begin with a clear vision of how new technologies can improve teaching and learning. Computers and the information superhighway can make significant contributions to a community's goals for education reform if they are an integral part of a comprehensive plan for school improvement. New technologies can enhance school readiness and help all students meet high standards. They can promote continuous professional development for teachers and foster greater parent and community involvement in education. They can reconnect students with their communities, they can smooth the transition from school to work, and they can help develop the lifelong learning skills students will need in our 21st century economy.

Industry may become an even stronger partner for education reform in response to careful planning and well articulated technology needs. Systemwide, and statewide efforts to establish clear education goals and challenging academic standards could help define what educators and families need from computers and the information superhighway. In such an environment, industry partners could assume a leadership role if they work to supply this market with user-friendly, low maintenance systems that are cost effective and easy to scale-up for widespread use.

A Challenge Grant application should make a convincing case that the proposed plan of action is likely to be an effective response to significant education need, and that the consortium partners are the appropriate ones to meet that need. Strong applications have a well defined concept—an idea for specific learning improvements— that clearly demonstrates how a new technology will be used to improve education.

To take a specific example, as part of the effort to ensure all children can read by age 8 or Grade 3, educators, business leaders and community organizations could form a consortium to develop new applications of technology to improve reading and literacy skills for young children. Becoming a competent, self-reliant reader by Grade 3 is essential to future academic achievement and later success in the work force. New technologies with interactive learning applications could give each child access to the power of one-to-one tutoring to improve reading. Computers and electronic networks could increase the participation of older students, and the effectiveness of parent involvement in literacy instruction.

To work with these technologies effectively, teachers and students need access to interactive computer applications and networked learning resources that can generate high quality content in all of the core subjects. The creation of this new content should be bolstered by continuous professional development for teachers and sustained support for students, that goes beyond the acquisition of generic computer skills to include mastery of technology applications specifically designed to improve academic achievement. Teachers and students must learn to seamlessly integrate these new learning tools into the curriculum. If this professional development and these technologies are embedded in the fabric of work in the school, the teachers and students themselves may participate in the creation of engaging new learning content that meets high academic standards.

In middle schools, for example, these powerful learning tools can increase student achievement in science and mathematics by elevating the content of instruction and the rigor of student work in these disciplines. It is clear from recent reports that more time on task is not enough. Middle school teachers can use these technologies to take students beyond simple problem solving to in-depth study of the scientific principles and underlying concepts behind the solutions. If they build on this learning through well-focused projects, high school students and teachers can use these tools to gain access to the power of scientific inquiry and mathematical reasoning at some of our best colleges, universities, research institutes, and scientific firms.

In this increasingly networked society, learners of all ages have an opportunity to work with an enormous wealth of knowledge. Teachers and students should be able to use telecommunications to overcome their isolation from a multitude of scholars and rich information resources that could help them improve education. With these tools they can collaborate with their colleagues in classrooms across the country to form new learning communities that no school system could develop on its own.

Linking middle school or high school students with college students and faculty may improve the preparation of young people for postsecondary education. Many students never consider a college education as a real possibility until they have a personal opportunity to become actively engaged with the life of these institutions. Computers and telecommunication networks can be used to strengthen the early preparation of students for college.

Professional development for teachers and the design of more rigorous content should be based on a careful analysis of the learning needs of students, and it should be consistent with the school's curriculum, mission, and professional standards. Teachers, administrators, parents, and community leaders should participate in decisions about the nature of the professional development and the content of the new learning activities.

A teacher's primary educational partners are the students' parents. When families and teachers are in effective communication, students stand a greater chance of success. If parents learn how to use technology effectively, they can bring a vast array of education resources to the home. Parents can extend the time and place for learning from the classroom to the living room, creating new opportunities for sustained study in core disciplines. With similar applications of technology, educators can forge new alliances with business leaders and local agencies that improve education by extending learning into the community.

Most of our students begin their careers directly after high school. These new technologies can be used to improve the transition from school to work. In a networked economy employers must have well-educated employees who make skilled use of information technologies to increase their knowledge and improve their productivity. If these new learning tools are embedded in the day-to-day work of the classroom, they will help students develop the skills they need for successful careers.

Technology Innovation Challenge Grants provide seed money to stimulate the development of promising learning technologies in specific communities. They generate fresh possibilities for software developers, cognitive researchers, education leaders and others to collaborate on the creation of a research-based generation of education software that uses recent advances in cognitive science to support improved learning. If their success is well documented, the most effective practices, and the important lessons drawn from their efforts, may receive widespread use in communities across the country.

*(continued)*

## Exhibit **10A.1** *Continued*

But Challenge Grant successes and lessons must be well documented. A carefully designed evaluation plan should be part of each application. It is not enough to promise that an evaluation will be done at some point in the future. A specific section of the application should explicitly describe the evaluation design that will be in place when the grant begins. The plan should establish clear benchmarks to monitor progress toward specific goals, and it should be explicit about how improvements in learning and instruction will be assessed. Developing evidence of effectiveness should not be put off until the last stages of the effort. In a Technology Innovation Challenge Grant, a strong evaluation plan must be a consideration from the design stage onward and information generated by the evaluation should provide continuous feedback for improvement to the project and to the wider education community.

### Selection Criteria

During the Summer of 1997, external panels of experts will review applications in a three tier process, and make recommendations to the Secretary of Education. The review panels are generally composed of individuals representing three broad perspectives: (1) teachers who use new technologies in the classroom; (2) administrators with school-wide or system-wide responsibilities for developing effective applications of technology; and (3) researchers and consultants drawn from universities, hardware manufacturers, software developers and telecommunication firms. The Secretary will use two criteria to select applications for funding: "significance" and "feasibility". Is it important and can it be done?

**Significance** will be determined by the extent to which the project:

1. offers a clear vision for the use of technology to help all students learn to challenging standards;
2. will achieve far-reaching impact through results, products, or benefits that are easily exportable to other settings and communities;
3. will directly benefit students by integrating acquired technologies into the curriculum to improve teaching and student achievement;
4. will ensure continuous professional development for teachers, administrators and other individuals to further the use of technology in the classroom, library, or learning settings in the community;
5. is designed to serve areas with a high number or percentage of disadvantaged students or other areas with the greatest need for educational technology; and
6. is designed to create new learning communities among teachers, students, parents, and others, which contribute to State or local education goals for school improvement, and expand markets for high-quality educational technology or content.

**Feasibility** will be determined by the extent to which:

1. the project will ensure successful, effective, and efficient uses of technologies for educational reform that will be sustainable beyond the period of the grant;
2. the members of the consortium or other appropriate entities will contribute substantial financial and other resources to achieve the goals of the project; and

3. the applicant is capable of carrying out the project, as evidenced by the extent to which the project will meet the problems identified; the quality of the project design, including objectives, approaches, evaluation plan, and dissemination plan; the adequacy of resources, including money, personnel, facilities, equipment, and supplies; the qualifications of key personnel who would conduct the project; and the applicant's prior experience relevant to the objectives of the project.

In the final award of grants under this program, the Secretary may also consider the extent to which each application demonstrates an effective response to the learning technology needs of areas with a high number or percentage of disadvantaged students or the greatest need for educational technology. Sweeping, unsubstantiated claims about the number of low income students or high need communities to be served should be avoided. A well documented plan for meeting specific education needs in these schools and communities should be presented.

### Eligible Applicants

Applications must be developed by a consortium including at least one local educational agency with a high percentage or number of children living below the poverty line. The application must be submitted by a local educational agency, but a single educational agency is not eligible to apply unless it is part of a consortium that may include other local educational agencies, private schools, state educational agencies, institutions of higher education, businesses, academic content experts, software designers, museums, libraries, or other appropriate organizations.

During 1995 and 1996, a total of 43 Challenge Grants were awarded to LEAs in communities across the country. Although these 43 LEAs are not encouraged to reenter this competition as primary applicants, they may consider participating as members of consortia in which other LEAs are the primary applicants. In such cases they are expected to demonstrate that they are not duplicating or overextending work under their current grant.

### Definition of a Local Educational Agency (LEA)

An LEA is defined as follows in Title XIV, Part A, of the Elementary and Secondary Education Act, as amended: ". . . a public board of education or other public authority legally constituted within a State for either administrative control or direction of, or to perform a service function for, public elementary or secondary schools in a city, county, township, school district, or other political subdivision of a State, or for such combination of school districts or counties as are recognized in a State as an administrative agency for its public elementary or secondary schools." The law states further: "The term includes any other public institution or agency having administrative control and direction of a public elementary or secondary school."

In other words, a local educational agency (LEA) is an entity defined under state law as being legally responsible for providing public education to elementary and secondary students. In some states this may include, under state law, an entity performing a service function for public schools, such as an intermediate service agency (ISA). The application must be submitted by a single LEA, but the LEA is not eligible to apply unless it is part of a consortium.

*(continued)*

## Exhibit **10A.1** *Continued*

### How to Apply

Application Deadline: May 30, 1997

Each submission should be concise and clearly written. Each submission should include the five sections of the Application and the six sections of the Appendix listed here.

### The Application

Each application should have the following five sections:

1. **Title Page:** Use the Title Page form included in these guidelines or a suitable facsimile to cover each application copy.
2. **Table of Contents:** Include a one-page table of contents.
3. **Abstract:** Attach a one-page double-spaced abstract following the Title Page (this is in addition to the abstract requested on the Title Page itself). The abstract should mention the problem or need being addressed, the proposed activities, and the intended outcomes.
4. **Narrative:** Although a standard outline is not required, in a narrative of no more than 25 double-spaced pages, printed in 10 point font or larger, you should address the selection criteria and the issues discussed in this application package.
5. **Budget:** Use the attached Budget Summary form or a suitable facsimile to present a complete budget summary for each year of the five-year project. Please provide a justification for this budget by including, **for each year,** a narrative for each budget line item, which explains: (1) the basis for estimating the costs of professional personnel salaries, benefits, project staff travel, materials and supplies, consultants and subcontracts, indirect costs, and any projected expenditures; (2) how the major cost items relate to the proposed activities; (3) the costs of evaluation; and (4) a detailed description explaining the funding provided by members of the consortium. Please include project staff travel funds for two trips during each year of the project to Challenge Grant Project Directors' meetings in Washington, D.C.; and two trips during each year of the project to regional Challenge Grant meetings. Each trip will be for three days for up to three persons. At these meetings each Challenge Grant recipient will have an opportunity to strengthen its efforts by collaborating with the other grantees funded in this program.

### The Appendix

Each application should be accompanied by an appendix which includes the following six numbered sections:

1. **List of Consortium Members:** List all consortium members, their contact persons, addresses, telephone numbers, and fax numbers. Similar information should be provided for other sources of support. The roles and contributions of all consortium members should be described clearly within the 25-page narrative. Letters of commitment should be included in this section of the appendix to clearly document the role and contribution of each member.
2. **Project Personnel:** Please provide a brief summary of the background and experience of key project staff as they relate to the specific project activities you are proposing.

3. **List of Application Authors:** Please list all persons who wrote the application, their organizational affiliation, the sections they worked on, and the approximate percentage of the total effort each one contributed.
4. **Evidence of Previous Success:** Include a brief summary of any evaluation studies, reports, or research that may document the effectiveness or success of the consortium or the activities proposed in the narrative section of the application.
5. **Equitable Access and Participation:** Section 427 of the General Education Provisions Act (GEPA) requires each applicant to include in its application a description of proposed steps to ensure equitable access to, and participation in, its federally-assisted program. Each application should include this description in a clearly identified section of the appendix. The statute, which allows applicants discretion in developing the required description, highlights six types of barriers that can impede equitable access or participation: gender, race, national origin, color, disability, or age. You may use local circumstances to determine the extent to which these or other barriers prevent equitable participation by students, teachers, parents or other community members. Your description need not be lengthy, but it should include a clear and succinct description of how you plan to address those barriers that are applicable to your circumstances, and it should support the discussion of similar issues in the narrative section of the application.
6. **Private School Participation:** Private schools may participate in Technology Innovation Challenge Grant applications as consortium members. However, if they do not participate as consortium members, Section 14503 of the Elementary and Secondary Education Act of 1965, as amended, (20 U.S.C. 8893) requires that a Technology Innovation Challenge Grant recipient shall, after timely and meaningful consultation with appropriate private school officials, provide private school children and teachers, on an equitable basis, special educational services or other program benefits under this program. Section 14503 further requires LEAs and educational service agencies to consult with private school officials during the design and development of a Challenge Grant application. Each application should include a specific section in the appendix which describes the consultations that have taken place, and the proposed plans for addressing the needs of private school children and teachers, should a Technology Innovation Challenge Grant be awarded.

### Other attachments
**Other attachments are not encouraged. Reviewers will have a limited time to read each application. Their consideration of the application against the selection criteria will be limited to the five sections of the Application and the six sections of the Appendix listed above. Supplementary materials such as videotapes, CD-ROMs, files on disks, commercial publications, press clippings, testimonial letters, etc. will not be reviewed and will not be returned to the applicant.**

### Proprietary Information
Applications may contain innovative technical or business ideas that, if released to the public, could reasonably be expected to cause substantial competitive harm to the consortium member that submitted that information. Bold legends clearly identifying information that a consortium member believes is of a proprietary nature should appear at the top and bottom of each page on which it appears. The U.S. Department

*(continued)*

## Exhibit 10A.1 *Continued*

of Education will take this designation into account in determining whether this information can be released in response to a Freedom of Information Act request.

### How to Submit Applications

**The deadline for receipt of applications is May 30, 1997. All applications must be received on or before that date.** This closing date and procedures for guaranteeing timely submission will be strictly observed.

### Number of Copies of the Application

All applicants are required to submit one (1) signed original and two (2) copies of the application (including one unbound copy suitable for photocopying). Each copy of the application must be covered with a Title Page (form included in these guidelines) or a reasonable facsimile. All applicants are encouraged to submit voluntarily an additional four (4) copies of the application to expedite the review process. Applicants are also requested to submit voluntarily three (3) additional copies of the Title Page itself. The absence of these additional copies will not influence the selection process. **All sections of the application and all sections of the appendix must be suitable for photocopying to be included in the review (at least one copy of the application should be unbound and suitable for photocopying).**

### Mailing Address, and Address for Applications Sent by Commercial Carrier

Technology Innovation Challenge Grants ATTN: 84.303A
U.S. Department of Education Application Control Center
Room 3633 Regional Office Building-3
7th & D Streets, S.W. (D Street, S.W. Entrance)
Washington, D.C. 20202-4725
Telephone: 202-708-8493

**Applications sent by mail must be received no later than May 30, 1997.** Applications not received by the deadline date will not be considered for funding unless the applicant can show proof that the application was (1) sent by registered or certified mail not later than five (5) days before the deadline date; or (2) sent by a commercial carrier not later than two (2) days before the deadline date. The following are acceptable as proof of mailing: (1) a legibly dated U.S. Postal Service postmark, (2) a legible mail receipt with the date of mailing stamped by the U.S. Postal Service, (3) a dated shipping label, invoice, or receipt from a commercial carrier, or (4) any other proof of mailing acceptable to the Secretary.

    **Applications delivered by hand** before the deadline date will be accepted daily between the hours of 8:00 a.m. and 4:00 p.m., Eastern Time except Saturdays, Sundays, or Federal holidays at the Application Control Center, U.S. Department of Education, Regional Office Building 3, Room 3633, 7th and D Streets, S.W., Washington, D.C. (Telephone: 202-708-8493). **Applications delivered by hand on May 30, 1997 (on the deadline date) will not be accepted after 4:00 p.m., Eastern Time.**

### Notification of Award

Applicants will be notified by September 30, 1997 whether their application is being funded.

## Assurances and Certifications

Applications selected for funding will require a signed Form ED 80-0013 ("Certifications Regarding Lobbying; Debarment, Suspension and Other Responsibility Matters; and Drug-Free Workplace Requirements"), Standard Form SF 424B ("Assurances—Non-Construction Programs"), and Standard Form LLL ("Disclosure of Lobbying Activities") before an award is made.

## The Forms

The following forms are required in all applications. They may be photocopies as necessary.

- Title Page Form
- Budget Summary Form

OMB No. 1810-0569 Form Exp.: 3/ 00

## TECHNOLOGY INNOVATION CHALLENGE GRANTS

According to the Paperwork Reduction Act of 1995, no persons are required to respond to a collection of information unless it displays a valid OMB control number. The valid OMB control number for this information collection is 1810-0569. The time required to complete this information collection is estimated to average 80 hours per response, including the time to review instructions, search existing data resources, gather and maintain the data needed, and complete and review the information collection. If you have any comments concerning the accuracy of the time estimate(s) or suggestions for improving this form, please write to: U.S. Department of Education, Washington, DC 20202-4651. If you have comments or concerns regarding the status of your individual submission of this form, write directly to: Technology Innovation Challenge Grant Program, U.S. Department of Education, Room 606D, 555 New Jersey Avenue, NW, Washington, DC 20202-5544.

This application should be sent to: No. 84. 303A
U.S. Department of Education
Application Control Center
Room #633, ROB-3
Washington, D.C. 20202-4725

**1. Application No.**

**2. Employer Identification No.**

**3. Legal Applicant (local educational agency)**

**4. Project Director**

Legal Applicant Name
Address (Complete)

Name and Title
Address (Complete)

Congressional District(s)

Telephone: _____  _____
Fax: _____  _____
Area Code    Number

*(continued)*

### EXHIBIT **10A.1** *Continued*

**5. Federal Funds Requested:**

| | |
|---|---|
| 1st Year \_\_\_\_\_ | 4th Year \_\_\_\_\_ |
| 2nd Year \_\_\_\_\_ | 5th Year \_\_\_\_\_ |
| 3rd Year \_\_\_\_\_ | TOTAL \_\_\_\_\_ |

**6. Consortium Members (other than Legal Applicant):**

Fill in NUMBER of each.

| | |
|---|---|
| \_\_\_\_ Other LEA | \_\_\_\_ Inst. of higher ed. |
| \_\_\_\_ SEA | \_\_\_\_ Other non profit |
| \_\_\_\_ Library | \_\_\_\_ For profit firm |
| \_\_\_\_ Museum | \_\_\_\_ Other |

**7. Duration of Project**

Starting Data: \_\_\_\_\_
Ending Date: \_\_\_\_\_
Total Number of Months: 60

**8. Student Population Directly Benefiting**

from the Project per Year

**9. Number of Teachers Directly Benefiting**

from the Project per Year

**10. Application Title**

**11. Brief Abstract of Application: (Do not leave this blank)**

**12. Certification By Authorizing Official**

The applicant certifies to the best of his/her knowledge and belief that the data in this application are true and correct and that the filing of the application has been duly authorized by governing body of the applicant.

Name _____ Title _____ Telephone _____

Signature _____ Date _____

TITLE PAGE FORM
Instructions for Completing Title Page Form
**DO NOT FORGET TO HAVE THE FORM SIGNED**

**ITEM 1. LEAVE BLANK—FOR OFFICE USE ONLY**
**ITEM 2. EMPLOYER IDENTIFICATION NUMBER:** Enter the unique 12-digit number assigned to your organization called the Federal Identification Number. It can be obtained from your budget office. NOTE: No grant can be awarded without a Federal Identification Number. If you do not have one, you should initiate the process to obtain one by calling Ms. Kim Nguyen at (202) 708-9268.

**ITEM 3. LEGAL APPLICANT:** Enter the name and complete mailing address of the local educational agency which will serve as the legal applicant (fiscal agent). When more than one institution or agency is involved, enter the name of the one which will be responsible for budget control. NOTE: Acknowledgments of grant awards are sent to this address. Remember to complete this section fully.

**ITEM 4. PROJECT DIRECTOR:** Enter the name and complete mailing address of the Project Director or Co-Directors (fiscal agent). If no one has been selected, so indicate and enter the name of the person who can be contacted to discuss the programmatic aspects of the project. NOTE: Name and address listed here will be used to mail notifications of application status. Do not forget to include the telephone number. Both this address and the Legal Applicant address should be detailed. Remember to complete this section fully.

**ITEM 5. FEDERAL FUNDS REQUESTED:** Enter the amount of Federal funds being requested in each year of the project. Under "TOTAL" enter the cumulative amount requested for the duration of the project.

**ITEM 6. CONSORTIUM MEMBERS:** Include the number of each type of consortium member organization included in the consortium.

**ITEM 7. DURATION OF THE PROJECT:** Enter appropriate starting and ending dates.

**ITEM 8. STUDENT POPULATION DIRECTLY BENEFITING FROM THE PROJECT PER YEAR:** Simple student count as of Fall 1996 will suffice.

**ITEM 9. NUMBER OF TEACHERS DIRECTLY BENEFITING FROM THE PROJECT PER YEAR:** Enter the number of teachers.

**ITEM 10. APPLICATION TITLE:** Self-explanatory.

**ITEM 11. BRIEF ABSTRACT OF APPLICATION:** Keep concise and confined to the space provided, but in no case should you leave this blank. Also see instructions under "How to Apply: Application Content" for submitting a separate one-page abstract.

**ITEM 12. CERTIFICATION BY AUTHORIZING OFFICIAL:** Enter the name, title, and telephone number of the official who has the authority both to commit the Legal Applicant to accepting Federal funding and to execute the proposed project. **Submit the original ink-signed copy of the authorizing official's signature.**

## 5 Year Budget Summary

Budget Item

| | Requested | YEAR 1 Support by LEA or other sources | Total |
|---|---|---|---|
| A. Direct Costs | | | |
| 1. Salaries (professional & clerical) | _____ | _____ | _____ |
| 2. Employee Benefits | _____ | _____ | _____ |
| 3. Employee Travel | _____ | _____ | _____ |
| 4. Equipment (purchase) | _____ | _____ | _____ |
| 5. Materials & Supplies | _____ | _____ | _____ |

*(continued)*

### Exhibit **10A.1** *Continued*

|  | YEAR 1 | | |
|---|---|---|---|
|  | Requested | Support by LEA or other sources | Total |
| 6. Consultants & Contracts | _____ | _____ | _____ |
| 7. Other (equip. rental, printing, etc) | _____ | _____ | _____ |
| 8. Total Direct Costs | _____ | _____ | _____ |
| B. Indirect Costs | _____ | _____ | _____ |
| TOTAL | _____ | _____ | _____ |

|  | YEAR 2 | | |
|---|---|---|---|
|  | Requested | Support by LEA or other sources | Total |
| A. Direct Costs |  |  |  |
| 1. Salaries (professional & clerical) | _____ | _____ | _____ |
| 2. Employee Benefits | _____ | _____ | _____ |
| 3. Employee Travel | _____ | _____ | _____ |
| 4. Equipment (purchase) | _____ | _____ | _____ |
| 5. Materials & Supplies | _____ | _____ | _____ |
| 6. Consultants & Contracts | _____ | _____ | _____ |
| 7. Other (equip. rental, printing, etc) | _____ | _____ | _____ |
| 8. Total Direct Costs | _____ | _____ | _____ |
| B. Indirect Costs | _____ | _____ | _____ |
| TOTAL | _____ | _____ | _____ |

|  | YEAR 3 | | |
|---|---|---|---|
|  | Requested | Support by LEA or other sources | Total |
| A. Direct Costs |  |  |  |
| 1. Salaries (professional & clerical) | _____ | _____ | _____ |
| 2. Employee Benefits | _____ | _____ | _____ |
| 3. Employee Travel | _____ | _____ | _____ |
| 4. Equipment (purchase) | _____ | _____ | _____ |
| 5. Materials & Supplies | _____ | _____ | _____ |
| 6. Consultants & Contracts | _____ | _____ | _____ |
| 7. Other (equip. rental, printing, etc) | _____ | _____ | _____ |
| 8. Total Direct Costs | _____ | _____ | _____ |
| B. Indirect Costs | _____ | _____ | _____ |
| TOTAL | _____ | _____ | _____ |

| | **YEAR 4** | | |
| | Requested | Support by LEA or other sources | Total |
|---|---|---|---|
| **A. Direct Costs** | | | |
| 1. Salaries (professional & clerical) | _____ | _____ | _____ |
| 2. Employee Benefits | _____ | _____ | _____ |
| 3. Employee Travel | _____ | _____ | _____ |
| 4. Equipment (purchase) | _____ | _____ | _____ |
| 5. Materials & Supplies | _____ | _____ | _____ |
| 6. Consultants & Contracts | _____ | _____ | _____ |
| 7. Other (equip. rental, printing, etc) | _____ | _____ | _____ |
| 8. Total Direct Costs | _____ | _____ | _____ |
| **B. Indirect Costs** | _____ | _____ | _____ |
| **TOTAL** | _____ | _____ | _____ |

| | **YEAR 5** | | |
| | Requested | Support by LEA or other sources | Total |
|---|---|---|---|
| **A. Direct Costs** | | | |
| 1. Salaries (professional & clerical) | _____ | _____ | _____ |
| 2. Employee Benefits | _____ | _____ | _____ |
| 3. Employee Travel | _____ | _____ | _____ |
| 4. Equipment (purchase) | _____ | _____ | _____ |
| 5. Materials & Supplies | _____ | _____ | _____ |
| 6. Consultants & Contracts | _____ | _____ | _____ |
| 7. Other (equip. rental, printing, etc) | _____ | _____ | _____ |
| 8. Total Direct Costs | _____ | _____ | _____ |
| **B. Indirect Costs** | _____ | _____ | _____ |
| **TOTAL** | _____ | _____ | _____ |

**Note: Items 1 through 7 are budget line subtotals that are to be described in the Detailed Budget.**

## Application Package Checklist

**APPLICATIONS MUST BE RECEIVED NO LATER THAN MAY 30, 1997**

CHECK:

- The Application Title page has been completed according to the instructions on the back of the title page.
- The Application Title page has been signed and dated by an authorized official and the signed original has been included with your submission.

*(continued)*

EXHIBIT **10A.1** *Continued*

- **SUBMIT ONE ORIGINAL PLUS TWO COPIES OF THE APPLICATION AND THE APPENDIX (INCLUDING ONE UNBOUND COPY SUITABLE FOR PHOTOCOPYING), PLUS FOUR VOLUNTARILY SUBMITTED ADDITIONAL COPIES. EACH COPY SHOULD INCLUDE THE FOLLOWING SECTIONS:**

**The Application:**

- the title page (page 1)
- table of contents (page 2)
- an abstract (page 3—one page maximum)
- a narrative (up to 25 pages double-spaced)
- the budget summary form, and a detailed budget justification

**The Appendix:**

- list project personnel
- list consortium members
- list application authors
- evidence of success
- equitable participation
- private school participation

**In addition to the above, include three (3) additional copies of the title page.**

**ADDRESS AND DEADLINE DATE:**

Technology Innovation Challenge Grants
ATTN: 84.303A
U.S. Department of Education Application Control Center
Room 3633, Regional Office Building-3
Washington, D.C. 20202-4725
Telephone: 202-708-8493

**REMEMBER: Applications mailed or sent by commercial carrier must be received by May 30, 1997.** Hand delivered applications must be received no later than 4:00 p.m., Eastern Time on May 30, 1997.

# RFP Analysis of Technology Innovation Challenge Grants 1997 Competition

### Hot Buttons

Of overriding importance is the general thrust of the project. The grantor wants to see a project that uses these three strategies or components or whatever you would like to call them: (1) development of interactive learning content, (2) continuous professional development, and (3) integration of new technologies into curriculum.

Phrases used to explain the grantor's vision: "modern communication centers for learning," "information age learning centers," "new learning centers."

Please note the following sentence, quoted directly from the request for proposal: "Applications in which the primary purpose is to equip schools, build networks, or obtain operating funds for existing systems have not been successful in this competition in the past." The grantor even went so far as to put the entire sentence in boldface type.

A consortium or community partnership is central to the grantor's vision.

The consortium need not be limited by geography.

Mentioned is that education and training can be brought into "every classroom, workplace, and home in the community at any time of day." This relates to the consortium (schools, businesses, and parents), and it relates to time shifting with the use of technology.

An applicant must propose a five-year project.

Grant will range in size from $250,000 a year to $1,500,000 a year. A yearly budget may not exceed $1.5 million.

Application must be submitted by an LEA (Local Education Agency) on behalf of the consortium. The LEA will be the fiscal agent.

Each consortium must have an LEA with a "high percentage or number of children living below the poverty line."

Project year one must include start-up activities including initial trials of new learning content and sustained professional development.

Project years two and three should be devoted to refinement and expansion of the new applications of technology.

Project years four and five should support system-wide adoptions that become self-sustaining after project year five.

The consortium must contribute "substantial commitments for the cost of equipment, technical support, network linkage, telecommunication services, and other resources."

### Proposal Content

1. Title Page
2. Table of Contents
3. Abstract
4. Narrative

   The proposal narrative that the grantor expects to receive requires the following parts:

   • Problem(s) statement(s)
   • Project objectives

- Project description
- Evaluation plan
- Continuation plan
- Dissemination plan
- Key personnel qualifications

Within the narrative parts listed above and in the appropriate places, the following must be shown:

- Documentation of "high number of disadvantaged students"
- The project must be designed to serve disadvantaged communities and citizens.

  Simply put, what this means is that if parental involvement with technology is expected, you cannot expect parents to pay for the technology. If you do, then only certain segments of society will be able to participate. This goes against one of the purposes of this competition.

- The project is replicable.

  Replicability has more to do with your problem and your circumstance than it does with the project. As long as the problem you are solving exists elsewhere, and as long as the circumstances you used to solve the problem also exist elsewhere, then the project is replicable. In other words, if you have a unique problem or a unique solution, your project is not replicable. Yes, your project needs to be innovative, but not unique.

- A consortium (partnership) exists in reality.

  While an LEA serves as the official applicant and fiscal agent, the LEA is applying on behalf of a consortium of involved and committed partners.

  This consortium is not a "nice to have" item. The existence of a working consortium is absolutely essential to getting funded.

  Analysis of last year's funded applicants shows the average number of consortium members in a winning project to be eleven (11).

  The point of this consortium is to develop "new applications of technology to transform factory era schools into information age learning centers."

  Possible consortium members include (in addition to an LEA)
  - Higher education
  - State education agencies

- Private schools
- Research institutes
- Libraries
- Museums
- Telecommunications firms
- Software developers
- Hardware manufacturers
- Entertainment producers
- Other businesses
- Other appropriate community organizations

Specific objectives for active participation by each consortium member at each stage of project development is expected by the grantor.

- Not necessarily part of the consortium, but just as necessary is involvement of parents. The grantor expects to see parents integrally involved. Note this sentence from the RFP: "A teacher's primary educational partners are the students' parents." The point here seems to be to involve parents via the new technology. Exactly how is up to you.

- The consortium must contribute substantial resources to the project.

  The grantor expects to see specific contributions "clearly identified and documented." Clearly identifying contributions means just that. Say specifically what the contribution of a consortium member is. Do not use generalities.

  To *document* means to get a letter of commitment (sometimes called a letter of support) from each consortium member setting forth the concrete contribution(s) of the member. These letters should be written by you. At the very least, you should give each consortium member a set of points to include in the letter if they write it themselves.

- Technology is integrated into curriculum.

- Professional development is ongoing.

- "New learning communities" are created.

  The concept of a learning community is not limited by geography. In this context, community does not have the traditional meaning of a locality, but rather a learning community is a confluence of like-minded groups and individuals who use modern telecommunications technology to ignore physical distances.

  Interestingly, and concurrently, the grantor also wants to ensure that traditionally underserved (low-income) communities (the old meaning) within the applicant's geographical area receive benefits from the new applications of technology.

- That your organization is capable of actually doing the project you describe.

  The simplest way to show organizational capability is to describe related projects that you have successfully completed in the past.

- A time line that agrees with this basic organization:

  - Project year one—Start-up activities, including trials of new learning content and professional development

  - Project years two and three—Refinement and expansion of the new applications of technology (including students and professional development)

  - Project years four and five—System-wide adoptions of the new applications of technology

  - Project year six and beyond—The project becomes self-sustaining. (This means that the continuation plan is very important. It always is in a grant proposal, but in this case the grantor has been very specific. We ignore a continuation plan at our peril.)

- Describe your consultation with private school officials during the design and development of your project.

- Describe the ways in which the project will address the needs of private schoolchildren and teachers.

**5.** Budget

Use Budget Summary form included in RFP

Use one form for each of the five project years

Include funds for two trips during each project year for project personnel to meetings in Washington, D.C. (three days for three people)

Include funds for two trips during each project year for project personnel to regional meetings (three days for three people)

Include a narrative with each year's Budget Summary form, including the following:

- Basis for estimating the costs of salaries, benefits, travel, materials, supplies, consultants, subcontracts, indirect costs, and any other projected expenditures

- How the major cost items relate to the proposed activities

- Costs of evaluation

- Detailed description of funding provided by members of the consortium (in kind)

*Appendix*

1. List of Consortium Members
2. Project Personnel
3. List of Application Authors
4. Evidence of Previous Success
5. Equitable Access and Participation
6. Private School Participation

*Publishing Requirements*

1. Table of Contents is one page.
2. Abstract is one page, double-spaced.
3. Narrative limited to 25 double-spaced pages.
4. All text is in 10-point font or larger.
5. Budget forms may be a "suitable facsimile." This means you may recreate the budget forms using your computer.
6. The Appendix sections must be numbered as shown.
7. No attachments other than those requested should be included.
8. Deadline for receipt of applications is 4:00 P.M. May 30, 1997.
9. Deliver application package to:
   Technology Innovation Challenge Grants ATTN: 84.303A
   U.S. Department of Education Application Control Center
   Room 3633, Regional Office Building-3
   7th and D Streets, SW (D Street, SW Entrance)
   Washington, DC 20202-4725
10. Submit a signed original of the proposal.
11. Submit two complete additional copies of the proposal.
12. Voluntarily submit four additional copies of the proposal (what a grantor "encourages," interpret as "commands").
13. Voluntarily submit three additional copies of the Title Page.
14. Therefore, a complete application package includes a complete original proposal with original signatures, six complete copies, and three additional copies of the Title Page.

*Questions*

1. What constitutes a "high number or percentage of disadvantaged students?"

2. What statistics are sufficient to prove a high number of disadvantaged students?

3. What constitutes a "greatest need for educational technology"?

4. What statistics are sufficient to prove a need for educational technology?

5. What is the "three-tier process" mentioned for proposal review?

6. When the proposal mentions "products," does it mean that we may partner with a for-profit company, thereby using grant funds to help develop a product that will eventually produce profits for the company?

7. Roughly what percentage of the total project budget should be in-kind contributions from the consortium referred to as "substantial financial and other resources."

8. Is it acceptable to submit a job description in the place of a key personnel bio if we intend to hire the person with grant funds.

9. If we follow our Title I guidelines with respect to involving private schools, will we meet the requirements of this application?

# Chapter 11

# When, Who, What, Where, and How Much?

## *Expanding the Project Outline*

The next step is to expand the project outline you started earlier in Chapter 10. There are 6 key components to this outline:

- Step 1: The approach (the How). Flesh out the rough outline you just made by adding in the intermediate steps and major tasks. Use the Expanded Project Outline form to record your work. Use the Expanded Project Outline Form provided on the disk. If necessary, use the Task Sheet also provided.
- Step 2: Time lines (the When). Go through your expanded outline and determine how much time it will take to do each step. Fill in the blanks on the Expanded Outline Form by each item in the outline.
- Step 3: Human resources needed (the Who). Go through the expanded outline and determine what staff will be needed to do each step. Fill in the blanks on the Expanded Outline Form by the appropriate items in the outline.
- Step 4: Other resources needed (the What). Go through the expanded outline and determine what equipment, materials, supplies, and services will be needed to do each step. Fill in the blanks on the Expanded Outline Form by the appropriate items in the outline.
- Step 5: The facilities needed (the Where). Go through the expanded outline and determine where each step will take place. Fill in the blanks on the Expanded Outline Form by the appropriate items in the outline.

• Step 6: Expense (the How Much). Assign a cost to each resource needed. Fill in the blanks on the Expanded Outline Form by the appropriate items in the outline.

As much of the project has been expanded in previous steps, this chapter will focus on how to plan the project time frame, resources needed, and project costs in some depth.

### Time Frame

You probably have a good idea how long it will take to get from where you are now to "go." If your project is a study or research project of some sort, then it has a definite beginning and ending. If not, then it is the end date that first needs to be determined. After all, the project will be a success and the time frame for its end will be years down the road. What then does the grantmaker expect?

Think about the grantmaker's purpose. The grantmaker wants to see if your project is successful enough at solving the problem (in which you are both interested) to be initiated in another location. The grantmaker wants to be able to evaluate your progress at a certain point when the results are apparent. Therefore, time frame means the first time valid short- to midterm results can be measured. Sometimes, this means the project is designed as a three-month project, a year-long project, a five-year project, or more. In the longer projects, results are measured in stages. In the shorter projects, results are measured as if the project has a finite beginning and ending. You will continue your project and you will continue evaluating it and reporting or publishing results, but for purposes of grant funding, you need to set a time frame for a benchmark evaluation and subsequent report of results.

As we expand the project outline, think in terms of benchmark results for each component when you are setting time frames. You will not likely know the exact date of the end of your project. You will have to estimate. Give yourself enough room to operate effectively, but make a decision. (Working from an outline makes it much easier.) Unless the grantmaker specifies otherwise, time frames should be looked at in terms of project months. This way, if funding is held up a month or two, you are not stuck with an out-of-date schedule. Your proposal should be detailed enough to be a project management plan in and of itself. If the time frames are not calendar dated, but listed relative to when the project starts (as in project month one), then the management plan is easier to follow.

### Resources Needed

When you do a project, you bring to bear all manner of resources, most of which many people leave out of grant proposals. It is a fact that as many people are turned down by grantmakers for underestimating what they need as are turned down by overstating their case. After all, if you do not even know what you need to fully operate your project, how can you be expected to succeed? From the grantmaker's point of view, you need to know exactly what you must have to effectively operate your project.

Resources can be anything from flesh and blood to, well, flesh and blood. We will need people—project leaders, support staff, researchers, teachers, managers, bookkeepers, mentors—different types of people depending on the project. If you were doing a medical or health research project, you might need flesh and blood, right? The resources you need—the tools you need—are driven by the project's needs.

As you plan your project, it is important that you include everything you need, not just the things you are going to ask for from the grantmaker. It is a major mistake not to make a complete list. Most grantmakers ask for the entire project budget and then a smaller budget-within-a-budget itemizing your funding request. Grant funding does not support the entire budget of a project. Grant funders want to see your investment. It proves your commitment to making the project work, as well as to continuation. Most grantmakers want to see a financial or in-kind investment by other project partners as well. The subjects of continuation and in-kind will be discussed in detail later on in this book.

### Project Costs

Now all that remains is to cost out the resources you need. It is vital to cost out every single thing you will need for a project as realistically as possible. Why? Because many an organization has nearly been broken by the awarding of a project in which not all the costs were figured. After all, who eats the surprise costs? The organization does if it does not want the project to fail. There are many horror stories, such as the school that realized its technology dreams through a grant that slipped through with the reviewers not questioning the fact that there were no funds built in for wiring and necessary renovation to handle the technology installation. It cost that school district tens of thousands of dollars it did not have to correct the error. On a less dramatic note, what about all the projects that simply eat and breathe secretarial support, when no accounting for such support has been made in the budget? Just how much additional work can your support staff take? It is very important to carefully think through the resources needed and their cost. Again, a good project outline will protect you from serious errors.

## EXPANDING THE OUTLINE—AN EXERCISE

1101.DOC

### Step One: Rewrite the Project Outline on the Expanded Project Outline Template

Go back to your project outline. Look it over carefully to ensure that you have included all main steps, substeps, and major activities. Add and revise as necessary. Then, enter your outline onto the leftmost column on Expanded Project Outline Template provided on the disk. Use as many template sheets as you need. Enter one step every third line. Do not double up steps. Give yourself plenty of room.

### Step Two: Check Time Frame on Expanded Project Outline Template

To the right of each step you have listed, put a check mark in the appropriate box under the heading Time Frame. For now, just estimate how long it will take to do each step individually in terms of weeks. Later, a time line will be created for the entire project.

### Step Three: List the Human Resources Needed and Their Cost on Expanded Project Outline Template

To the right of each step you have listed, write down every job function needed to implement that step. Start over with each step. Even if you have already listed a job function under another step, relist it if it is needed. By job function is meant teacher, project coordinator, support staff, researcher, volunteer mentor, technician, systems engineer—you do not need to name names.

Beside each job function, approximate their annual salary or hourly rate. Regarding volunteers, list a salary they would be paid if you were to pay them. To help you with this part of the task, there are books of wages and salaries on the bookshelf in your local library or large bookstore. Look in the business section. Again, you are just approximating at this point.

### Step Four: List Other Resources Needed and Their Cost on Expanded Project Outline Template

To the right of each step you have listed, write down other resources you will need to accomplish the step. Include supplies, materials, reference books, computers, printers, satellite dishes, test tubes—anything you can think of. Guestimate the cost of these items in the space to the right. Guestimates should include a factor for installation and wiring. We are just looking for ballpark amounts at this stage.

### Step Five: List Facilities Needed and Their Cost on Expanded Project Outline Template

To the right of each step you have listed, under the appropriate heading, write down the facilities needed. You have to house the project even if only in one classroom in a school or one room in a recreation center. Under cost, enter your best guess at the cost to rent the space and maintain it. A quick check with your local Chamber of Commerce on the cost of rental space in your community or information about overhead costs from your organization financial officer will tell you what you want to know.

### Step Six: Tally the Approximate Total Project Cost

Finding a matching funder involves a matching interest in solving a problem, as previously discussed. It involves having a fundable, well-developed project. It also involves matching the project cost with an appropriate funder. It is important to approach a funder with an appropriate funding request. You should not approach a funder who usually funds $25,000 projects with a $500,000 request. Similarly, you do not want to approach a $500,000 funder with a $500 request.

Use the information you have recorded on the Expanded Project Outline Template to tally three figures. First, quickly add all the cost figures your organization is likely to fund or donate to the cause. Next, add all the cost figures a partnering organization is likely to fund or donate to the cause. Finally, add together all the costs you need to request from a grant funder.

## Making Some Key Decisions

It is time to look at the stages of the grant's process that have been completed.

- Broad Problem identified
- Real Problem narrowed down
- Real Problem designed
- Project outlined

- Funder researched and chosen
- Funder's guidelines requested and received
- Three outlines made from the guidelines: proposal content, publishing requirements, and sales points

The next critical step is to develop the project to the depth required to attract the funder. Determine the details about which a winning proposal will be written.

Grantseekers often express dismay at all the work involved to prepare to write the proposal. However, you have to approach the problem from the grant giver's perspective: Is it likely that you would risk $5,000, $25,000, or even only $500 on a stranger's good idea? Would you do it if your job and business depended on the results? Would you do it if you had to answer to your board for your decision? What about if you have 20 more proposals from people who have really developed their project in depth? Would you risk the funds on the good idea or on one of the well-developed projects? Which would you prefer? If you look at this from the funder's viewpoint, it is apparent that you would want to see detailed plans before you would make a decision. Beware. One never gets something for nothing—at least not something good. One does not get grant funds for a few hours of brainstorming. It takes patience and time, as well as teamwork.

Remember, once there is a well-developed project, many proposals can be written to support various subprojects or parts of it. Each proposal is different, depending on the funder to whom you are writing, but projects are constant, though evolving. All your work is worth it, for many winning grant proposals can come out of it. No one funder will fund every cent needed for a project. They will expect an investment from you and from partners, if not in cash, in in-kind. Funders do like to team on a project, however. Having more than one funder on a project is an asset, not a detriment.

This section focuses on the further development of the project. The better developed the project, the more likely a proposal will attract the attention, and funding, of the grantmaker.

## *Corroborate Your Problem Statement*

The first focus of further development is the problem statement. In Part I of this book, we listed the evidence we had on hand that the problem we're addressing is a valid one for our target population. Refer to page 28 (Step Eight of the design section), if you need to refresh your memory. Follow the four steps below to gather the corroborating evidence.

1. Review the list you made previously. Make additions or changes.

2. If your project is a complex one, multiyear or multicomponent, you might need help from a team member to gather the information. Remember, research is the area most easily delegated. ▦ 0501.DOC

3. Perform the research.

4. Place copies of the information gathered in the Project Notebook. This information will be used to write the problem statements (needs analysis) sections of your proposals.

## Determine Project Precedents

Your project design should be solidly founded according to the prevailing knowledge and wisdom of your field. However, the funder is rarely, if ever, an expert in your field. Even if you are applying to your own state department, the reader may not have a specialty in the issue you are addressing, so you must provide evidence that your project plan is viable. A major way of doing this is to cite precedents. Of course, you are not likely to find a project exactly like yours—you are trying to be innovative—but there should be projects with elements similar to components of your project. If you have a mentoring component, for example, it should not be hard to find articles or studies indicating the positive effect of mentoring. The project may not be identical, but the general topic of mentoring can be validated.

What references and sources would you use to find precedents for your project, and where would they be located? Where would you start looking? Professional journals normally carry articles about projects and studies in a given field. Does your professional library or public library have an index to a collection of the professional journal(s) related to your project? Computer search tools are usually available to search articles in periodicals by topic.

Recent texts and other books are possibilities. We stress the word *recent*. Proposals have been eliminated from competition because the references were out of date. Certainly, there are cases in which landmark studies are years old and these can be referenced, but the rule of thumb is to not use references that are more than three years old. If it is the year 2000, then 1997 is the oldest reference you should use. If your project is a highly technical project, a few months old may be the limit. Regarding references, the more current the better.

Clearinghouses are organizations that maintain information in a given field. There are clearinghouses that specialize in health-oriented information or education information. These clearinghouses usually have searchable databases that can be accessed directly or through the Internet.

Ask your reference librarian to assist you if you are not familiar with a clearinghouse in your project's field of study.

Professional associations usually sponsor studies and make available reports that can be acquired for a few dollars. Sometimes, the most recent information about a given subject can be obtained through a professional association.

The more technical and, generally, the greater the funding sought, the more need for project validation in the manner discussed here. Use the worksheet provided on the disk to record notes for your Project Notebook.

## Innovation and Hot Buttons

Innovation is a frightening word. Few feel they are truly capable of innovating. This is because the word *innovation* causes us to think we are expected to create something totally "from scratch." However, grantmakers use the word innovation to indicate that an organization cannot just continue business as usual and acquire grant funding to support it. Neither is the organization likely to be awarded a grant to do the same thing everyone else in the country is doing. Remember the purpose of most grant funding—to seed projects with a good chance of modeling a solution to a problem.

Grantmakers are looking for projects that spring logically from the problem—from trying to find a solution to a problem. They want to fund projects with a new twist or fresh turn to them. Rarely is anything truly brand new, unprecedented, developed. What is expected is serious thought and creativity evidenced in a workable project.

The following are some questions that may help you express the innovation in your project.

- Specify differences in your project and your normal programs.
- Describe how your project changes the usual way of doing things.
- Describe how your project could be called creative.
- Describe how your project is an improvement over other similar projects.
- Specify the fit between your project and your normal programs.

After you have answered the preceding questions, go back to the Hot Buttons Outline. Write a paragraph about how your project "pushes" each hot button. How does your project address each hot button issue? If a hot button is not addressed, and your project cannot be revised to include it, why is it not pertinent?

Use the worksheet provided on the disk to record your answers.

## Replication and Dissemination

The next things to think about in relation to your project are replication and dissemination. Replication means how your project can be useful to others. Do not make assumptions that the reader will "automatically" see how your project is useful outside your own context. It is important to position the project to its best advantage with the funder, and as the funder is usually looking for replicability, you need to point it out.

A second related issue is how to communicate information on the project to those who can use the information to set up a project of their own. This involves dissemination. Dissemination is usually the responsibility of the awardee, so the potential funder will need to know how you intend to publicize the program and what you will provide if someone asks for information.

It is not as hard as it sounds. The same clearinghouses from which you retrieved information also receive information. Usually, there is a set format for submitting information. Contact the clearinghouse and ask. In addition, there are the normal channels—professional associations and networks. Another easy way to provide information is through the Internet. Set up a project web page and you are set.

The following are some questions for guidance:

- List types of organizations that could use your project.
- What parts of your project can be used by these organizations "as is"?
- What parts of your project would have to be tailored to meet another organization's needs?
- What information could you provide to help others reproduce the project?
- Through what associations, networks, and clearinghouses are you going to spread information about your project?
- Are you going to publicize the project? If so, how?

## Continuation Plan

This is one of the most important topics in relation to fundability. An organization must be able to tell the potential grant funder how the project will continue after grant funding ends. This is not optional, it is mandatory. There is no point in seeking grant funding if your project will eternally be dependent on it. That is not the purpose of project grant funding—it is seed money to get you started.

This one topic causes more trouble than any other because there are so many misconceptions about grant funding. Everyone knows someone who works for a project funded by grant money and that project has been supported by grant funding for years—seemingly forever. In Part II there was a discussion of formula grant funding versus project grant funding. Those people that have worked "forever" under grant funding are working for a formula grant program, not a project grant program. This book examines writing proposals for competitive project grants, not applying for formula grants. Though a type of "proposal" (actually, an application is submitted for a formula grant program), it is not really a grant proposal. You get funds because of circumstances, not because of your creation of an innovative program.

With project grants, grantmakers will not make an award unless they are assured that if your project works, it will continue. Grantmakers want to fund projects that have the potential of long-term impact. The exception is the research project or study, where there is a definite ending. Therefore, do not write the proposal if it cannot be continued. Remember, you will be supporting only a small portion of the costs from year to year because most of the up-front costs will be covered by the grant. A grantmaker does not want to hear, "Well, after your funding runs out, we will just ask another grant funder for support." That is merely putting a bandage on the problem; it does not solve it.

The following are some questions for guidance:

- Will the project be self-sustaining after funding has ended? If so, how will it be sustained?
- Will the project earn income? If so, how?
- Is there other funding available to support the project once it is up and running?
- Are there local resources to support the program outside your organization? If so, how will you access those resources?

## Trouble-Shoot the Project

The next step is to trouble-shoot the project. It is important to think about potential problems. Some problems may be overcome through minor project redesign. Some problems are intrinsic to the project. These are the problems to watch out for so that they do not become more than just problems—so they do not turn into a disaster. If there are too many problems, of course, you need to rethink your project and do some further research and planning.

Sometimes, it is a good idea to tell the funder, in the proposal, of a potential problem. If the problem is one that represents a reasonable risk in relation to the project's ultimate expected result, then it is a good idea to include the description of the potential problem along with your safeguards and "just in case" plans. This impresses the grantmaker with your professionalism and the amount of thought you have put into your project. Then, if the reader notices the potential difficulty, he or she will know you know about it and are accounting for it in your project design.

Be sure to think of potential "political" problems. Who do you need to have on board? Who do you need to keep in the communications loop? Is there someone you should ask to be a partner just so things will run smoothly?

## Determine Resource Provisions

As previously discussed, no grantmaker will fund an entire project. The organization will have to cover a significant part of the budget. When reviewing the Expanded Project Outline, it can be noted that everything necessary to the project was included, not just the things wanted from the funder. In doing this, the organization accounted for the total project budget. A common mistake made by many grantseekers is to record only the things they want from the funder. This gets them into serious difficulty when they have to come up with matching funds or in-kind contributions. They do not know the needs of the entire project, and therefore they do not know the overall project budget. They focus on only a small part. Grantmakers want to see the entire project budget and then the portion for which you are requesting their support. It is easy to accomplish this if an Expanded Project Outline has been completed correctly.

The next step in the project development process is to divide up the responsibility for funding all the resources needed to support the project. Determine which resources your organization will provide, which resources a partnering organization will provide (if applicable) and the resources for which there has been a request for funding. Look back at the Amplified Project Outline. Costs for each item needed should have been included on the outline worksheets. These costs should be used to build your budget.

## DETERMINING RESOURCE PROVISIONS—AN EXERCISE

 1102.DOC

The following tools are provided as worksheets and can be used to complete budget planning:

- Resource Provisions forms
- Budget Worksheets for equipment, personnel, materials, supplies, services, travel, and facilities [See Exhibit 11.1 (1102.DOC) for an example of the specific worksheets.]
- Total Budget Summary
- Requested Budget Summary (For an example, see Exhibit 11.2.)

### EXHIBIT 11.1

### Budget Worksheet—Travel

| Funder | Item | Cost | Amount | No. People | Total |
|--------|------|------|--------|-----------|-------|
| **Example** | | | | | |
| C Foundation | Mileage | $ .23 per mile | 100 | 2 | $46 |
| C Foundation | Hotel | $85 per night | 3 | 2 | $510 |
| C Foundation | Meals | $50 per day | 4 | 2 | $400 |
| | | | | | |
| | | | | | |
| | | | | | |
| | | | | | |
| | | | | | |
| | | | | | |
| | | | | | |
| | | | | | |
| **Totals** | | | | | |

EXHIBIT 11.2

## Total Budget Worksheet Example Summary

| Item | Equipment | Personnel | Materials | Supplies | Services | Travel | Facilities | |
|------|-----------|-----------|-----------|----------|----------|--------|------------|--------|
| Modems | $500 | | | | | | | |
| Computer | $1200 | | | | | | | |
| VCR | $850 | | | | | | | |
| Cabinet | $100 | | | | | | | |
| Projector | $623 | | | | | | | |
| Desks | $435 | | | | | | | |
| Proj. Dir | | $32,000 | | | | | | |
| Adm. Asst. | | $21,000 | | | | | | |
| Textbooks | | | $747 | | | | | |
| Software | | | $342 | | | | | |
| Copy Paper | | | | $250 | | | | |
| Postage | | | | $290 | | | | |
| Pens/Paper | | | | $500 | | | | |
| Consultation | | | | | $600 | | | |
| Installation | | | | | $1200 | | | |
| Mileage | | | | | | $46 | | |
| Hotel | | | | | | $510 | | |
| Meals | | | | | | $400 | | |
| Field House | | | | | | | $100,000 | |
| Classrooms | | | | | | | $30,000 | |
| | | | | | | | | |
| | | | | | | | | **Total** |
| Subtotals | $3708 | 53,000 | 1089 | 1040 | 1800 | 956 | 130,000 | **191,593** |

# Chapter 12

# Mission, Goals, and Objectives

## *Mission Statement*

There are many words for mission. *Vision* and *long-range goals* are two of the most common. For grant projects, goals and objectives must be concrete and measurable—no fuzzy or lofty language. The Mission Statement is the place to explain the ultimate vision of how the world will be better as a result of the successful implementation of your project.

Mission Statements are "solution" statements; they should be stated in terms of the solution that is being sought. They are the "flip side" of problem statements. If the Real Problem has been clearly defined, the problem statement can be turned around so that the mission is the ultimate solution for that problem.

Exhibit 12.1 shows some examples of Mission Statement development.

Notice that in each case, the Mission Statement is broad and far reaching, much broader than the statement of the Real Problem. *Substance abuse in our community will be eliminated*. That is the ideal, but the total elimination of drug abuse and alcoholism is a bit beyond reach at this point in our society. It is fine to reach for the sky at the Mission Statement level. When defining goals and objectives, it will be more down to earth—a doable, measurable statement.

Look back at the Broad Problem in each example case. *Youth vandalism has skyrocketed in our community*. Now look at the Mission Statement. *Youth vandalism in our community will be eliminated*. Notice that it is the flip side of the Broad Problem statement. Our problem is that we have a lot of vandalism . . . our mission, therefore, is that we will have no vandalism. Is it realistic to say that you will have absolutely no vandalism?

## Exhibit 12.1

### Examples of Mission Statement Development

*Broad Problem*—Youth vandalism has skyrocketed in our community.

*Real Problem (a Probable Cause)*—(a) too little parental supervision, and (b) too little community supervision.

*Mission*—(action-statement of the problem focusing on target population).

**Youth vandalism in our community will be eliminated.**

*Broad Problem*—Children aren't getting immunized.

*Real Problem (a Probable Cause)*—(a) there's only one health clinic, (b) people live many miles from the clinic and most have no transportation.

*Mission*—(action-statement of the problem focusing on target population).

**All children will be immunized.**

It does not matter. How much vandalism do you want anyway? Your mission is to eradicate it entirely. In our model world, there is no vandalism.

In Exhibit 12.2 are some additional examples. Notice that some are lofty and fuzzy and some are more specific. This is a matter of taste, and the amount of specificity depends on the type of project you are working on. If you feel more comfortable putting a percentage on it, do so, but in cases in which the ultimate solution should be obvious, go ahead and strive for the best. The idea of a Mission Statement is to stretch.

## Exhibit 12.2

### Additional examples of Mission Statements

There will be no new incidents of tuberculosis.

No adult will be illiterate.

Ninety percent of the students in fourth, fifth and sixth grades will read at or beyond grade level.

All Pleasantville citizens will be drug-free.

Eighty percent of high school graduates will get training or further education after graduating.

## *Goals and Objectives—Introduction*

Writing goals and objectives seems to be one of the most difficult parts of developing a project and writing a proposal. The problem arises out of the differing opinions about the definition of a goal and an objective, and also because people tend to think that their own definition is the only correct one.

To illustrate the point, here is a list of words that, according to *Webster's Collegiate Dictionary,* are interchangeable: goal, objective, target, purpose, and intent. *Roget's Thesaurus* adds aim, design, ambition, and destination. Some organizations substitute *strategy* for *objective.* Some groups organize ideas by objective, then strategy, then activity. Some rank goals below objectives. Some refer to the lowest level under objectives as *tasks,* and others call that level *activities.* One national organization, in recognition of the problem, set concrete definitions for all their affiliates to follow. Just to complete the circle, look up *task* in a thesaurus and you will find *goal* as a substitute.

The bottom line to this discussion is that, in project development and proposal writing, it does not matter which words you use, as long as you clearly convey your meaning to the reader. Goals and objectives are ways of explaining what you want to do, for whom, and what result you intend. Writing goals and objectives is a way of organizing your project. Writing goals is much like making an outline.

Rarely do grantors define what they mean by goal and objective, because, whatever their own definition, they assume everyone has the same one. The way to ensure that you are communicating with the reader is to clearly explain your definition of a mission, a goal, and an objective so the reader knows what to expect. The ultimate purpose is to give the reader as much information as possible with which to judge the structure and value of your project. The best way to avoid problems is to eliminate any possibility of confusing the reader.

The following section describes a logical structure and clear definitions to help you develop goals and objectives. The model is one that combines accepted standards of business and industry as well as government agencies so that whether the proposal is going to a corporation, a foundation, or a federal agency, it will provide the grantor with a logical structure and enough information for the proposal to be judged fairly.

The important thing is to remember the grantor who is reading the proposal. You are trying to communicate with the reader. You cannot talk one on one with the reader and find out his or her definition. You can, however, give the reader your definition and model so you are both using the same terms. Exhibit 12.3 is an example of the definitions and the

EXHIBIT 12.3

**Mission, Goal, Objective, and Task Model**

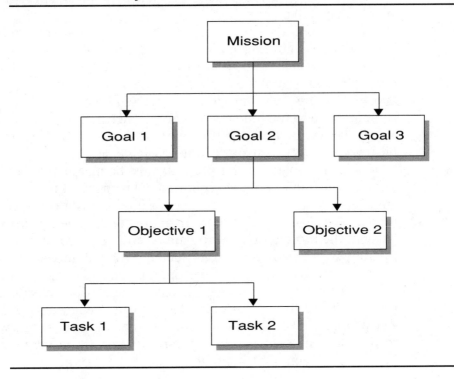

model. Feel free to create your own model, or feel free to use the one provided.

*Goals*

Goals are statements of the major steps to accomplish the mission of the project. This point can be confusing because of the way most people traditionally look at goals. As we have all grown up, we have learned that to be successful, one must set goals. We are told that appropriate goals are things such as: always be truthful . . . always try to be a good person . . . maintain a healthy lifestyle . . . never tell your wife her apple pie is not as good as Mom's . . . never compare your husband to your friend's boyfriend. All philosophically sound. All *law-giving* goals.

However, there are other, more far-reaching goals we are taught to set: every person will have at least a high school education, no children will go hungry, disabled people will be treated fairly, prejudice will be eliminated, educate the world to the danger of *E. coli* in uncooked food. All very worthy goals. All *policy-giving* goals. All *way-out-there* goals. *Some* are Mission Statement material.

Writing goals for a grant project is a different task. Your grant project has a definite beginning and ending. It is short term, by comparison to the law-giving goal or the policy-giving goal. What you are trying to do is set realistically attainable, measurable goals designed to get you to the end result—the solution—your project represents. You are trying to communicate to the funder your competence in doing the project. You are trying to paint a clear picture of what you are going to do to accomplish your project. You are writing *here-and-now* goals.

Goals and objectives for projects must be measurable and realistic. They are the framework to be followed in managing the project once the grant has been awarded. Remember, a proposal is a contract with the funder. The clearer you are and the more measurable the goals and objectives, the more protected you are regarding your result. If you have carefully worked out your project details and you implement your project as contracted through your proposal, you will do fine in the eyes of the funder, even if your project fails. Remember, the project is an experiment. You are attempting to implement a very educated guess to solve a Real Problem. You don't know for sure that all the elements will work, so you measure them as you go and try to learn from everything that is happening as you implement and evaluate your project.

## GOALS AND THE PROJECT OUTLINE—AN EXERCISE

 1201.DOC

Look back at your project outline. Remember that you first divided your project into the major steps that should be taken to accomplish your mission. These steps are listed at the roman numeral level of your outline. These steps represent the goals for your project. Look back at our peanut butter sandwich example in Chapter 4. What were the major steps in the outline?

I. Check to see what is in the pantry.

II. Purchase grocery items.

III. Make the sandwich.

IV. Eat the sandwich.

V. Were the desired results achieved?

VI. Clean up.

Look at those steps in terms of goals. What is it that we are actually doing?

**I.** Investigate resources (what is in the pantry?).

**II.** Get what is needed (purchase grocery items).

**III.** Put the project together (make the sandwich).

**IV.** Implement the project (eat the sandwich).

**V.** Evaluate the project (was it good?).

**VI.** Manage the project (clean up).

This is an excellent start. The project is organized into the major steps we will have to take to accomplish our mission (eliminate our hunger). However, these steps are not yet Goal Statements. Goals should be realistic, measurable, and clear. How is this accomplished?

*Realistic.*   Goals should be clearly achievable. Your mission is where you stretch. Your goals should be realistic and achievable. This does not mean they should be easy to achieve necessarily, but, remember, you are planning a project—you are not writing overall goals for improving the quality of life. The latter type of goals tend to be fuzzy and far reaching. Goals for a project should be an outline to the implementation and management of the project. They should be achievable.

*Measurable.*   Goals should be measurable. Measurability will be discussed in more depth later, but you must have some measure against which you can tell if you have accomplished the goal. If there is no measurement, you cannot tell what you have achieved. Measurement is expressed in terms of "how many" or "how much."

*Clear.*   Goal statements should be clear—no fancy language, no fuzzy words. Remember the reader. The reader has to be able to tell, at a glance, where you are going throughout your project from your goals. You should be able to take your goal statements to anyone at all, and he or she should be able to understand exactly what you are doing in your project.

*Five Parts.*   Goals have five parts. Goal statements should express the following:

- What you are going to do
- What approach you will use
- When you are going to do it

- For how many/how much (this is where you get in your measurement)
- What result is desired

This last part is critical: You should always state goals in terms of results. Goals for a project are not philosophical. You get to philosophize in the Mission Statement. Goals are practical steps to get that project done.

Look at each of the five parts individually.

**1. What You Are Going to Do**   The foundation of a Goal Statement is a "what" statement. It should be worded with an action verb— it should express activity. We have included a list of action verbs with the worksheets and templates included in this book to help you.

Look once again at our peanut butter and jelly example. What are we doing in each goal step?

  **I.** Investigate resources (what is in the pantry?).

  **II.** Get what is needed (purchase grocery items).

**III.** Put the project together (make the sandwich).

**IV.** Implement the project (eat the sandwich).

  **V.** Evaluate the project (was it good?).

**VI.** Manage the project (clean up).

In the first step, we are *assessing* our resources. Second, we will *acquire* the needed resources. Third, we *combine* or *organize* the project components. The fourth step is to *implement* the project. After implementation, the fifth step is to *evaluate* the results. The sixth step is one that should be added to every project—a management component. The sixth step is to effectively *manage* the project. Notice that every verb is an action verb. Every verb indicates that something is being done.

**2. What Approach You Will Use**   Many people have a definite problem with this section because *approach* or *methodology* (another word for approach) means something specific in their profession—it means something heavy with jargon. This is not what the funder means, so there is a communication problem on this portion of the development and of the proposal.

Methodology and approach are words that mean something very specific to some of us. We had whole methods courses devoted to it. We were taught to use the XZY method for this and the ABC method for that. Approach is a concept full of jargon to us. Now, reviewers are not usually or necessarily experts in the field represented by our project. You never know who the reader is going to be. They do not want to hear jargon. Universally, grantseekers get a lot of criticism from reviewers for our use of jargon, but it is partially because grantmakers do not know that in a way, they are really "asking" for it when they use the term *approach*. Read on to see what is really meant, in grantseeking terms, by approach.

What they want, very simply, is a step-by-step narrative, in English—lay language—of what we are going to do. That is it and nothing more. Just "We are going to do this first, this second, this third," and so forth. "We are going to hire staff, test children, develop curriculum, enroll children, teach curriculum, post-test, and evaluate."

Back to peanut butter and jelly. What approach are we using in each case?

**I.** Investigate resources (what is in the pantry?). Our approach is to look in the pantry and in the refrigerator.

**II.** Get what is needed (purchase grocery items). Our approach is to purchase goods needed.

**III.** Put the project together (make the sandwich). Our approach is to spread peanut butter on one slice of bread, spread jelly on another slice of bread, and then put the jelly and peanut butter sides together.

**IV.** Implement the project (eat the sandwich). Our approach is to put part of the sandwich in our mouth, chew, and swallow, and repeat.

**V.** Evaluate the project (was it good?). Our approach is to smack our lips, think about our tummy to see if it is full, and consider whether to make another sandwich.

**VI.** Manage the project (clean up). Our approach is to put lids on the containers, put the containers where they belong, and wipe up the counter.

Again, approach simply means how you are going to accomplish the goal. It is just a "how" question, nothing more or less.

**3. When You Are Going to Do It** The third part of a Goal Statement, the "when" component, is easy. When are you going to be working on this goal? You can state the "when" factor in terms of a specific month, or you can use the more general technique, "during project month two." If you have a goal that extends over the life of the project—our project management goal is an example—then you can say, "begins in project month one and extends for the life of the project." Or, you can simply say, "ongoing." Be careful; "ongoing" should not appear beside every goal. Goals are concrete, so for most goals, there should be a key month when most of the goal's activity takes place.

**4. For How Many/How Much**  Measurement. This is the critical part of any Goal Statement. Do not leave it out. If your goals are concrete, this measurement statement should not pose a problem. Instead of the peanut butter and jelly example, look at the counseling center example from Part I. What kind of measurability can you attach to each goal? We have listed some possibilities.

I. Establish a counseling center.
   Possibilities
   - To house two counselors, one support staff, and serve 15 clients a day
   - To serve 600 students annually
   - To serve 115 families in a three-county area

II. Enroll students.
   Possibilities
   - Enroll 35 students per month for the first six months of the project.
   - Enroll students monthly with a maximum of 20 served in any one month.
   - Enroll 100 students from three upstate counties.

III. Execute counseling program.
   Possibilities
   - For 200 students per year for three years
   - For 10 students in the first month, 20 in the second, and 15 per month for one year
   - For 100 families in the Pleasantville Community

IV. Monitor and evaluate counseling program.
   - Review records on each of 100 families.
   - Supervise two counselors and one support staff member.
   - Oversee individual programs for 40 students.

Again, if your goals are here-and-now goals, you should not have any problem with measurability. If you have problems, then re-think your goals. They're probably too vague.

**5. What Result Is Desired**  This is the most important part of the goal. Why do it if you do not have a target result? Grantmakers are intently focused on results. You must clearly state what you expect to happen if the goal is accomplished. Again, look at our counseling program example.

I. Establish a counseling center.

Results

- The building is ready for occupancy.
- The equipment is installed, working, and the offices are operational.

II. Enroll students.

Results

- The students are enrolled.

III. Execute counseling program.

Results

- 200 students are served.

IV. Monitor and evaluate counseling program

- The counseling program is run according to the best practices of ABC counseling.
- Students and families evaluate the program as being good or excellent.

As you can see, results are driven by the goal itself. In developing the results statement, ask yourself, "What do I want done, finished, or ready as a result of the successful completion of this goal?"

To help in formulating Goal Statements, we use a chart like the one in Exhibit 12.4. We have provided templates and further examples with this book for your use.

**Exhibit 12.4**

## Goal Statement Chart

| Do What? | Using What Approach? | By When? | For How Many or By How Much? | With What Result? |
|----------|----------------------|----------|------------------------------|-------------------|
|          |                      |          |                              |                   |

## Objectives

Objectives are the substeps needed to accomplish the goal, or the main steps. Using our peanut butter and jelly example, you can see how this works.

I. Investigate resources (what is in the pantry?).
   A. Check for peanut butter.
   B. Check for jelly.
   C. Check for milk.
   D. Check for bread.
   E. Make a list of things needed.

II. Purchase grocery items (get what is needed).
   A. Prepare to go to the grocery store and drive to store.
   B. Shop for needed items.
   C. Drive home.
   D. Unload groceries and carry them to kitchen.

III. Put the project together (make the sandwich).
   A. Open containers and prepare food.
   B. Get out tools.
   C. Make sandwich.
   D. Get liquid refreshment to go with sandwich.

IV. Implement the project (eat the sandwich).
   A. Prepare a place to eat sandwich.
   B. Consume sandwich and milk.

V. Evaluate the project (was it good?).
   A. Has hunger ceased?
   B. Is there a pleasant memory of the experience?
   C. Is there a good taste in the mouth?
   D. Is there a desire for another?
   E. Is the event worth repeating?
   F. Were the desired results achieved?

VI. Manage the project (clean up).
   A. Go into the kitchen.
   B. Put up containers of food.

C. Throw away the napkin.

D. Wipe the counter.

Objectives are the baby steps you take to accomplish the goal. They also have five parts, but there is a difference in objective statements. With objectives, you leave off how many/how much (you have already stated measurability in the goal) and you add by whom. Why? You want to start right now justifying staff requests. They are the most difficult ones to justify if you have not shown what responsibilities they will have up front.

You want the reader to say to him- or herself, "I cannot leave out the coordinator because then who will do these objectives (steps)?" How will the work get done? Putting the "who" in the objective justifies the staff needed to do the project and also gives you a chance to show where your own staff (your contribution) will be used. It gives you a chance to show your own staff commitment and volunteer involvement (advisors).

To help in formulating Objective Statements, we use a chart like the one found in Exhibit 12.4, modified on the disk to include objectives.

### Tasks

Below objectives in our hierarchy are tasks. For every objective, there are many tasks to be done to accomplish the objective. Tasks do not have to fit any particular format, and most (but not all) grantmakers will not require you to work through your project to this level of detail. However, you should use our process to develop a management and action plan for the project so the people involved know what to do. When you do this, you will take the project all the way down to the task level.

Go back to our example for illustration. The roman numerals are the goals, the letters are objectives, and the numbers are the tasks.

I. Investigate resources (what is in the pantry?).

   A. Check for peanut butter.

      1. Look in the cupboard.

      2. If found, open container and check amount in jar.

   B. Check for jelly.

      1. Look in the refrigerator for grape jelly.

      2. If found, open container and check amount in jar.

   C. Check for milk.

      1. Look in the refrigerator for milk.

      2. Open container and apply the sniff test—is it fresh and is there enough?

     D. Check for bread.

       1. Look in breadbox for white bread.

       2. Check for mold.

     E. Make a list of things needed.

II. Purchase grocery items (get what is needed).

     A. Prepare to go to the grocery store and drive to store.

       1. Get checkbook.

       2. Take car to grocery store.

       3. Get car keys.

       4. Open garage.

       5. Back out and take Main Street to grocery.

     B. Shop for needed items.

       1. Load cart.

       2. Pay cashier.

       3. Load groceries in car.

     C. Drive home.

       1. Start car.

       2. Take Main Street home.

       3. Enter garage.

       4. Close garage door.

     D. Unload groceries and carry them to the kitchen.

III. Put the project together (make the sandwich).

     A. Open containers and prepare food.

       1. Open peanut butter jar.

       2. Open grape jelly jar.

       3. Get out two slices of bread.

     B. Get out tools.

       1. Get two knives.

       2. Get out napkin.

     C. Make the sandwich.

       1. With one knife, spread peanut butter on one slice of bread.

       2. With the other knife, spread jelly on the other slice of bread.

3. Put the two pieces of bread together with the peanut butter and jelly sides together.

4. Put the sandwich on a napkin.

D. Get liquid refreshment to go with sandwich.

1. Get a drinking glass.

2. Get milk from the refrigerator, open, and pour into glass.

IV. Implement the project (eat the sandwich).

A. Prepare a place to eat sandwich.

1. Carry sandwich and milk to table beside favorite chair.

2. Sit in chair and put feet up on ottoman.

B. Consume sandwich and milk.

1. Pick up sandwich and take a bite, chew, and swallow.

2. Drink some milk.

3. Continue steps C and D until both the sandwich and milk have been consumed.

V. Evaluate the project (was it good?).

A. Has hunger ceased?

B. Is there a pleasant memory of the experience?

C. Is there a good taste in the mouth?

D. Is there a desire for another?

E. Is the event worth repeating?

F. Were the desired results achieved?

VI. Manage the project (clean up).

A. Go into the kitchen.

B. Put up containers of food.

1. Put the lids back on the jars.

2. Put the peanut butter in the cabinet.

3. Put the jelly in the refrigerator.

4. Put the cap on the milk.

5. Put the milk in the refrigerator.

C. Throw away the napkin.

D. Wipe the counter.

To help you task out your projects, a task worksheet is included on the disk.

## Conclusion

Part IV begins the phase of grantseeking that many people consider the only important part of grantseeking: proposal writing. In fact, writing the proposal is the least creative and the easiest of all the tasks in grantseeking—that is, if you have done everything as we have outlined it up to now. If you begin with proposal writing, you will still design a project. You will still fully develop a project. You will still analyze the request for proposal (RFP). You will do it all while you are writing the proposal, and, as a result, you will feel that proposal writing is really hard stuff. Doing everything all at once is hard; writing a proposal is not.

What we have done is break the overall task of grant seeking into manageable chunks in an understandable order, and we then further break these chunks into even smaller chunks or activities. For each activity, we create a data capture form. The outcome is that if you follow the order, answer the questions, and fill out the forms, you arrive at this point, ready to write a proposal.

You have a project fully developed. What is now needed to write your next proposal for this same project? All you need to do is find a funding source. Most of the work is already done. Once you go ahead and write the proposal about the project you have just completed, how much of the work toward a second proposal for a second funder have you already completed? The answer is that probably about 80 percent to 90 percent of the proposal is reusable. Yes, each funder gets its own proposal, but much of the material remains the same. It may be called something different. It may be in a different order. It may have to be slanted differently, but the basic material already exists.

It is this process that makes it possible for you to turn out 10, 20, or 30 proposals a year, thereby winning three, six, or nine grant competitions and bringing hundreds of thousands of dollars into your organization. Now you know the secret.

# Developing and Writing the Final Proposal

# Chapter 13

# Phase I: Problem Statement, Project Approach, Goals & Objectives, and Project

## *Introduction*

All grantseeking begins with a problem. Both development of a project and writing of a proposal start with a clear definition of a problem. Before writing a proposal, the project must be fully developed. An underlying assumption of this section is that you have already developed your project as outlined in earlier sections of this book. Exhibit 13.1 is a diagram of the work flow of the project, and will chart all the steps to a complete proposal. The first step, Problem Statement, has been highlighted.

## *Problem Statement—Introduction*  1301.DOC

Funders want to find projects that solve a problem. With the exception of local funding sources, they want to fund projects that can impact a given field regionally or nationally. How can this be accomplished? Regional and national impact is accomplished when a grantor provides money for a small project that can then successfully be modeled by others. State funders frequently want to seed programs that other organizations in the state can copy and implement. Local funders are the only ones really interested in simply supplying funds for your particular local organization. However, even these local funders want to see what problem is being solved with your project.

EXHIBIT **13.1**

## Workflow of Proposal Writing Process

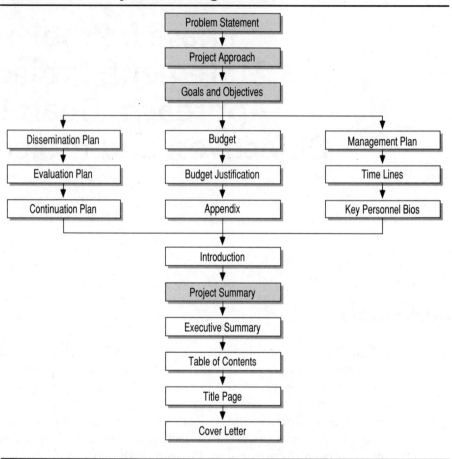

A critical point to be made about problems addressed in a grant proposal is to be sure that the focus is on your target population. Include the following in a proposal Problem Statement:

- A logical, narrative description of your problem
- Results of local needs assessments
- Historical data—how did this problem come about?
- Statement of the impact of this problem
- Statistical backup and comparisons about your problem

## *Problem Statement—Example*

Our district has a severe drop-out problem. Over XX percent of students drop out before graduation from high school. Our county has the highest drop-out rate in the state. The state drop-out rate is XX percent, which compares to a national average of XX percent.

One of the major reasons our students drop out is because their families see no need for their children to further their education. Most of our citizens belong to farming families (over 70 percent), who traditionally count on their children as a source of inexpensive labor, beginning as early as elementary age. Children at age 13 or younger are expected to work their family's farms; therefore, little time is left for education.

Farming is no longer providing the quality of life that it once was. Seventy-five percent of our families exist on incomes below 200 percent of poverty level (the measurement used by the Department of Family and Children's Services for public assistance). The average income for a family of five is $XX,XXX. To break the cycle of poverty in our area, family attitudes must be changed.

In a survey of 157 families, 67 percent of the heads of household said that graduation from high school was not one of their major priorities for their children. The list below shows the summary priority list from survey results. The survey listed 10 things from which to choose, numbered 1 through 10, with 1 being the most important to the person being surveyed as related to his or her children and 10 being the least important. Persons who could not read were administered the survey verbally. Items are listed in order from those that received the most response to those receiving the least response.

| Category | Number of Citizens |
| --- | --- |
| Total Baldwin County Population | 6,508 |
| Income about 200% of poverty level | 1,626 |
| Income at 151%–200% of poverty level | 885 |
| Income at 100%–150% of poverty level | 1,003 |
| Income at poverty level and below | 2,994 |
| Total below 200% of poverty | 4,882 |

| Area | % Below 200% of Poverty |
| --- | --- |
| Baldwin County | 75.1% |
| State | 14.7% |
| National | 13.1% |

*Survey Priorities*

1. Know how to farm.
2. Know how to keep house.
3. Know how to tend animals.
4. Know how to drive a tractor.
5. Know how to sell produce and/or livestock.
6. Know how to buy goods to run the farm.
7. Go to church.
8. Tend other children.
9. Graduate from high school.
10. Get a job.

Since farming can no longer support several family groups, the children who drop out quickly find themselves caught up in the cycle of poverty. Just a few years ago, the land could provide an excellent quality of life. Several generations farmed the same land at the same time, raising their families to follow them in the same honorable profession. Now, families who count on the family farm to support themselves and their children's children are subsisting at a lower and lower standard.

Citizens of this county are isolated. Most have never been outside the county. The nearest urban area (population 25,000) is in neighboring Wade County, more than 100 miles from the nearest community in Baldwin county. Because of their isolation, parents of the children in our schools do not know what kind of life their children could have outside this area, with education and support from them as well as from community role models.

Attitudes change slowly. In a county similar to ours in Tennessee, a program was instituted to raise awareness of the problems outlined above. Though the program had little impact during the first two years; after five years, high school graduates increased from 42 percent of the student population to 78 percent. The overall income level in the county has increased, and more and more citizens are becoming involved in the school system. There is a summary of results from this Tennessee project, entitled *Educating Our Way Out of Poverty*.

Numerous isolated rural communities across the country face the same problems we do. Our project uses some of the elements of the Tennessee program, with the addition of integral involvement of grass roots leaders. We have identified these leaders and have held two meetings with them to discuss the drop-out problem and its concrete consequences to the children of this county. With the help of these leaders, an incentives program will be developed for both the youths at risk of dropping out and for their families, thus going to the root of the problem.

### Tips for Creating a Good Problem Statement

- Always relate the problem to your target population.
- Don't get carried away and bring in extraneous problems—focus your efforts toward one well-defined problem
- Be careful not to simply state opinions—use opinions only when they are widely (nationally) accepted truisms; otherwise, back up your statements with statistics.
- Quote the funder's own research and statements when possible.

The next step is to create a Project Approach and Project Summary. Note that the Project Summary is not written until after several other components are finished. The workflow within this section to create a Project Approach involves three steps:

1. Develop a Mission Statement (see Chapter 12)
2. Develop a Project Outline (see Chapter 11)
3. Develop a Project Approach

Much later, a Project Summary will be written.

## Mission Statement

A Mission Statement flows from the Problem Statement. The Problem Statement sets out the problem. The Mission Statement turns the problem around and positively asserts that the purpose of the project is to provide a solution to the problem. They are "solution" statements.

Included in a Mission Statement are the following:

- A restatement of the problem in terms of solving or fixing the problem
- Emphasis on the target population
- The ultimate result the project is to accomplish

For examples of Mission Statements, see Chapter 12.

### *Tips for Creating a Good Mission Statement*

- Keep it general; specifics belong in the goals and objectives.
- Keep it short, preferably one sentence, two at the most.
- Make it an action statement, using active, positive verbs.

## *Project Outline—Introduction*

Using the forms provided in this book and the directions in Chapter 12, create an outline of your project.

- An outline is a systematic representation of content and organization.
- An outline must cover (explain) the project adequately.
- An outline must be arranged logically.
- The information at the roman numeral level (I, II, III, IV, etc.) describes the major steps to take to accomplish the mission (purpose) of the project.
- The information at the capital letter level (A, B, C, D, etc.) describes the steps to take to accomplish the major steps described in the roman numerals.
- The diagram in Exhibit 13.2 below graphically shows the logic flow in a project outline.

## *Project Approach—Introduction*        1302.DOC

This section can also be called Project Methodology or Project Description. Whichever title is used, there is no magic in what is wanted—a step-by-step description of your project from start to finish. Funders want to know exactly how you intend to set up and implement your project. Approach the Project Description as if you already have the money—you've been awarded the grant. What is the first thing you would do, the second, the third, and so forth? Obviously you do not have enough space, and the reader does not have enough time, for you to describe every small detail of your project, but all the major steps must be there. If you skip or leave out important steps, the reader will wonder if you know what you are doing. And, yes, the "story" of your project will be repeated—at least three times—once in the Project Summary, again in the Project Approach, and a third time in the Goals and Objectives.

EXHIBIT **13.2**

**Project Outline**

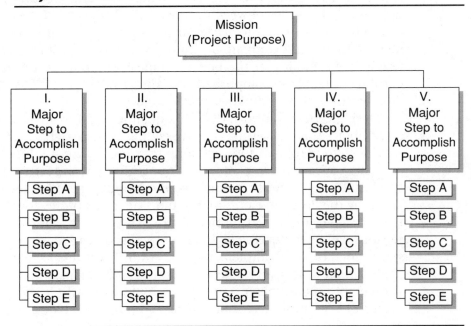

Include the following in a Project Approach:

- Statement of purpose and a two- to three-sentence overview of your project
- A step-by-step description of what you are going to do from start to finish
- Any major milestones in your project
- The roles of key personnel
- With each step you describe, note the time frame within which the step will be accomplished
- Justification of your approach

## *Project Approach—Example*

The proposed project, Storytime for Toddlers Pilot Study, is designed to be implemented throughout the library system of Rhode Island. Specially trained staff and volunteer parents from each library will develop and publish special lesson plans to introduce disadvantaged children to age-appropriate reading, listening, comprehension, and creating thinking skills through a series of weekly story hours. The focus of these sessions is on children in the 4-to-7 age range. A pilot program will be implemented to test and compare beginning and ending skill levels of a representative sampling of the target group of children. Recruitment and enrollment will be accomplished according to the Praytor Model by the Program Coordinator and designated library staff.

During program month (PM) 1, a qualified staff member from each of 42 libraries, along with a parent residing within each library service area, will be enrolled in a week-long training course produced by the National Education Association for Young Children and Literature. After successful completion of coursework, five two-day planning sessions will be led by the Program Coordinator and a qualified professional Instruction Designer, hired with project funds. The objective of the planning sessions will be to develop eight lesson plans to be used in a pilot eight-week program, to be implemented in PM 6. These lesson plans will include a pretest, learning objectives and detailed plans, and a post-test. Participant learning retention from week to week will be measured by means of a Stallford Retention XX test administered by trained parents as each child arrives for each story hour.

After the results of the Pilot Study are gathered and evaluated (during PM 8), the professional Instructional Designer will lead a second round of five two-day planning sessions to review results, revise the existing eight lesson plans and devise an additional eight lesson plans according to the results from the Pilot Study. Teams composed of designated library staff and parents will continue the planning session for three days to complete the remaining 34 lessons.

During PMs 9 and 10, all 50 planned lessons will be submitted to an Instructional Review Board made up of members of the State Library Council, the State Commission on Education, local Department of Education and Department of Special Education staff, and the professional Instructional Developer for final review and revision.

During PMs 10 and 11, the Instructional Review Board will develop a list of resource materials and equipment necessary to the implementation of the Storytime for Toddlers program. Based on the results, suggestions, lists and the conclusions of this committee, a model program will be designed and published during PM 12. At the same time, all information will be submitted for distribution and use throughout the nation via the National Educational Research Network Dissemination Program.

Based on the results of all studies and planning sessions and on the subsequent model program, implementation of a statewide Storytime for Toddlers effort, to be funded by State Library Education funds in combination with local and regional Health and Human Services Early Intervention funds, is projected to begin within three months of dissemination of pilot study information.

### Tips for Creating a Good Project Approach

- Write your goals and objectives first. They will provide an outline of your project from which to write the approach.
- Be sure your process is logical. Have a person who knows nothing about your project read this section; the outside "reader" should fully understand what you are going to do and be able to explain your project clearly from reading the Project Approach.
- If there is space, mention advisory board members, your own staff, and others whose time and effort will be "donated" to the project. The Project Approach is one place in the proposal that you can show your organization's level of commitment to the project.
- Do not use jargon in describing your project. Remember, readers may or may not be experts in the subject addressed by your project
- This is a how-to-section; you are simply answering the question, "How do you intend to do your project?"
- Back up your approach with descriptions of similar programs that have been successful in producing the results you desire.
- Be concise but thorough—use short, simple sentences.

## Project Summary—Introduction  1303.DOC

The Project Summary alternately may be called synopsis or abstract. Normally, a funder will limit the length of the Summary either by number of words allowed, or by telling you the Summary can be no longer than one page or a half page. If the funder does not give you guidance on length, keep the Summary to no more than one page—less if possible. Fully describe your project in other sections of the proposal. Your summary should provide a very concise, clear snapshot of your project in simple, straightforward terms.

Include the following in a Summary:

- A logical, chronological description of the essence of your project, including only major events
- Any events or components required by the funder should be mentioned briefly to show compliance.

• If you are requesting any major budget items (any items that make up a significant part of your budget), their use should be mentioned in the Summary.

## Project Summary—Example

A current, successful project, Project Hard to Serve (HTS), provides the basis for the proposed Go Forward project. Project Hard to Serve is a joint venture amount 14 local and regional agencies to educate disadvantaged individuals to the level of a general equivalency diploma (GED). The project has graduated 30 people to date, primarily female heads of households. With a GED, graduates are employable in minimum wage jobs that do not provide high enough income for self-sufficiency. The proposed Go Forward project will carry graduates of the HTS project a step forward to successful completion of their education and then to employment with wages high enough for self-sufficiency.

The first component of Go Forward provides a special education program that focuses on development of personal, professional, and communication skills. The program will be delivered in a workshop format with instruction by qualified members of the community including people from business and industry, graduates from the Chamber of Commerce Leadership program, and high school and technical college instructors. Twenty-four workshops will be held.

The second project component provides a series of business and industry tours so that participants can see various types of jobs available, meet potential employers, and learn about the requirements of the jobs from the people actually supervising and doing the work. Before and after each tour, a discussion session will provide an opportunity to answer questions and expand on the observations during the tours. Twelve tours and discussion sessions will be held.

Perhaps the most important part of Go Forward is the mentoring program. After enrollment, each participant will be matched with a mentor from the community to answer questions and provide a role model and guidance while the participant is involved in training, tours, and also while enrolled in coursework. An Individual Development Plan, including personal and professional goals and objectives, will be formulated by each participant with help from a licensed counselor and the mentor.

After the specialized workshops and tours, participants will be assisted in enrolling in their chosen course of study. Mentoring and counseling continue until graduation. On graduation from coursework, students will be placed in jobs.

Fifteen participants will be involved in the pilot project, with another 30 to be enrolled one year after the first group begins the program. During the first five years of project operation, over 200 participants will be enrolled. The mission is that at least 90 percent will complete all coursework necessary to gain at least an associate degree and will be placed in jobs providing adequate subsistence.

### Tips for Creating a Good Project Summary

- Be brief, but descriptive—you have a very small amount of space in which to tell your story.

- Write your summary last. As you develop the other parts of your proposal, some things will evolve and change—your summary must match your final draft.

- Adhere to limits. If there is a word limit, stick to it. If there is a page limit, do not cheat; do not expand margins, reduce type size, or otherwise try to get around the limits set by the funder. Rewrite and tighten your verbiage to fit the limit.

- Realistically, not all readers will read all portions of your proposal; however, the Summary is always read; if you present a fuzzy picture of your project in your Summary, the reader will get the impression that your project is not well thought out.

## Goals and Objectives—Introduction  1304.DOC

This section contains directions for creation of one of the 18 pieces of a grant proposal. You should have roughed out the goals and objectives during project development. This section should be an exercise in refining and polishing.

Creation of goals and objectives seems to be one of the most difficult parts of developing a project and writing a proposal. The difficulty exists in part because of the differing opinions about the definition of a goal and an objective, and because each person tends to think his or her own definition is absolutely the only correct one.

To illustrate the point, we just have to look up the word "goal." *Webster's Collegiate Dictionary* shows the following words as interchangeable: goal, objective, target, purpose, and intent. *Rogét's Thesaurus* adds aim, design, ambition, and destination. The bottom line is that in proposal writing it does not matter which word or definition you use, as long as you clearly convey your meaning to the reader. Goals and objectives are ways of explaining what you want to do, for whom, and what result you intend. Writing goals and objectives is a way of organizing your project.

Writing goals and objectives is actually fleshing out an outline of your project.

Rarely do funders define what they mean by goal and objective. This is because, whatever their own definition, they assume everyone has the same one. The way to insure you are communicating with the reader is to clearly explain your definition of mission, goal, and objective, so the reader knows what to expect. Use the terms that the funder uses. If the funder asks for strategies, then rename your goals as strategies to comply with the funder's terminology. If the funder asks for a "few broad objectives," then rename your goals to comply. Do not get hung up on words. Each level—goal or objective—is simply the steps it will take to accomplish the purpose of the level above it.

Include the following in a Goal Statement:

- What you are going to do and how you intend to do it
- Quantification of when, and for how many, or by how much
- Statement of results you expect

Include the following in an Objective Statement:

- What you are going to do and how you intend to do it
- Quantification of who will do it and when
- Statement of results you expect

Further examples of good goals and objectives can be found in Chapter 12.

### Tips of Creating Good Goals and Objectives

- Develop a chart and fill it out. The chart can be used "as is" in your proposal unless the funder requires otherwise.
- Even if the funder requires you to write out goals and objectives (not put them in chart form), fill out the charts. You should know all the information in the chart before you try to write goal statements or describe your project
- If you have to write out goal statements, keep the language and the sentence structure simple; write your goal statement in more than one sentence if necessary to make it clear. Remember, you are trying to communicate clearly to the reader.
- Have an outsider read your goals and objectives to see if he or she understands your project; if not, your statements are not simple and clear enough or do not follow a logical progression.

- Your goals and objectives must provide a clear and unambiguous map to your project.

## Tasks

Task are the very specific, small steps taken to accomplish objectives. At the task level, responsibility for the task, identification of resources needed, cost, and dates of accomplishment are assigned.

Most funders will not require task-level detail; however, if you are awarded a contract, the Task Analysis is likely to be required for large, multiyear projects for which a high level of funding is requested.

# Chapter 14

# Phase 2: Dissemination Plan, Evaluation Plan, Continuation Plan, Management Plan, Time Lines, and Key Personnel Biographical Sketches

## *Introduction*

The six proposal parts in this section can all be worked on concurrently after the Project Approach and Goals and Objectives are completed. As can be seen in Exhibit 14.1, there is no particular order in which these should be written, though they all need to be completed before you go on to the summations and final proposal parts. All of these parts should have been developed in the exercises in Chapter 11, and the writing of the proposal should put the final gloss on them.

## *Dissemination Plan—Introduction*  1401.DOC

Most funders (all but the very local ones) aim to test and establish projects that can be replicated by others. The idea is to provide funding for a model project that can grow and spread and ultimately positively impact education, health care, or the arts. These funders ask that you provide assurance in your proposal that you will see that information about

EXHIBIT 14.1

**Proposal Work Flow**

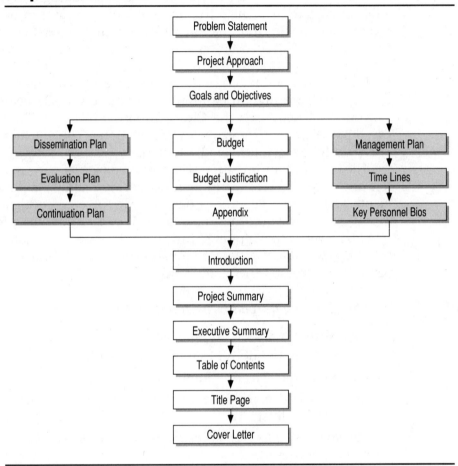

your project is shared broadly. Include the following in the Dissemination Plan:

- Specific avenues for disseminating information: statewide, professional, regional, and national
- A brief discussion of the types of information you will share.
- A description of any products that may be sold

## *Dissemination Plan—Example*

The ABC project is designed to be a model program for those serving disadvantaged, bilingual children, from first grade through fourth grade.

To ensure that others are aware of the project and know where to get information about duplicating it, our regional Young Child At-Risk Association has agreed to publish regular articles about progress. The Association's newsletter is mailed to every K–6 Administrator in our six-state region. Additionally, information will be disseminated statewide through the Administrator's Association and the Association of Teachers of Young Children.

National dissemination of project information will be accomplished through the Clearinghouse on Bilingual Education, 2355 North Street, Northwoood, Kentucky; the Clearinghouse on At-Risk Children, 4444 East Street, Eastwood, Oregon; and the National Young Child Network, 5555 South Street, Southwood, Montana.

The following information will be shared with anyone requesting it, free of charge: Project Descriptions, Budget Summaries, Staffing Requirements, and Progress Reports. Copies of the lesson plans, evaluation tools, tapes, templates, and other materials will be available for a fee of cost plus 20 percent plus shipping. Any funds generated from sale of materials will be separately accounted for and will be used for materials to expand the project to other grade levels.

### Tips for Creating a Good Dissemination Plan

- Use existing networks and newsletters.
- Write articles to publish in professional journals.
- Use appropriate clearinghouses.
- Cover your costs for disseminating extensive information—charge copy costs at least.
- The Polaris *Grantseeker's Guide to Resources* lists many of the National clearinghouses.

## Evaluation Plan—Introduction

 1402.DOC

Many funders require that a formal evaluation plan be included in the proposal. Even if a plan is not required, you should explain to the reader how you intend to judge whether or not your project was a success. Are you going to pretest and post-test students to determine progress? Will your project be a success if a certain number of students graduate . . . enter counseling . . . get a job? Will your project be a success if a certain number of patients are cured?

It is important to include a summary of the available evidence of your accomplishment of goals and objectives. The Evaluation Plan Worksheet which can be found in Exhibit 14.2 and on the disk (  1402.DOC) can act as a guide. Suppose one of your goals is to assess all eighth graders to determine their exact level of mathematics competency. Evidence of accomplishment of your goal could include: a copy of the test(s) used, compilation of test results, and your analysis of the test results.

## Exhibit 14.2

1402.DOC

### Evaluation Plan Worksheet

Using the worksheet below, write down a project goal and beside it, its objectives. Beside each objective, in the column headed "Evidence," list the documents, committees and other indicators of the accomplishment of the objective.

Example:

| Goal | Objectives | Evidence |
|------|-----------|----------|
| Institute a group drug counseling program for 1,000 people by FY 02 | Acquire appropriate staff to include 1 director, 2 counselors, and 1 support person | Ads for the positions Applications and employment records |
| same | Set up community advisory committee with members from health, social, education, and business sectors | Committee membership roster |
| same | Determine enrollment procedures | The written procedures |

| Goal | Objectives | Evidence |
|------|-----------|----------|
| | | |
| | | |
| | | |
| | | |
| | | |
| | | |
| | | |
| | | |
| | | |
| | | |

Other types of evaluation may be required by the funder. A fiscal audit may be a requirement. Even if the funder does not state that a fiscal audit will be done, assume it will. Be sure your accounting of the use of the money awarded is clear, accurate, and is documented properly.

For very large awards, an outside measurement may be required. In this case, you would hire an outside team of experts to come in and study your project and its progress and compose a report. If an outside assessment is required by the funder, you will be allowed to include the cost for it in your budget request.

Include the following in an Evaluation Plan:

- A listing of proof of accomplishment of goals and objectives. Items of proof can include: meeting agendas and minutes, results from tests and evaluations, enrollment and attendance records, employment records, committee rosters, and internal reports and memos.

- Accurate financial records that match the approved budget for the project—financial records should meet the standards of normal accounting practices.

- Reports should be done periodically to document project progress and future plans—expected publishing dates for these reports should be stated in the evaluation plan.

## Evaluation Plan—Example

### Goal 5

The students in our middle schools (1,500 students) will improve to or beyond grade level math competency by March 1999, as a result of the use of new instructional programs.

*Evaluation Plan.* Students will be pretested, using the IconTell, NoHyde Ratings, and Cheatem tests. Results will be recorded and kept in each individual's project file. In addition, the Barbearic Behavior Questionnaire (BBQ) will be administered to determine subject attitudes.

Guairanteed Gnuage Model (GGM) instruction program documentation will include lesson plans for each class, an example of each set of materials developed, a thorough description of instructional methodology, a weekly record of individual student progress, examples of student work, and notes from each weekly teacher–student meeting, as well as transcripts of grades from each student's other classes.

At the end of the project, subjects will be retested, using the same tests used for pretesting, and the BBQ will be administered again. The results from the pretests and post-tests will be compared with each other and the desired results of Goal 4.

### Goal 6

The project will be fully and appropriately equipped and equipment will be properly installed by March 1998.

**Evaluation Plan.** The Fiscal Officer, along with the Project Coordinator, will adhere to state purchasing requirements to acquire and install equipment. Purchased equipment will be installed according to all pertinent operation and safety codes. Equipment will be inventoried and will be used strictly for project purposes as summarized in this proposal and required by the funder. The annual outside audit will include evaluation of equipment purchase, installation, and use. The resulting audit report will be submitted to the funder in January of 2002 and 2003.

### Tips for Creating a Good Evaluation Plan

- Put together an internal evaluation team with the responsibility of tracking the project, doing reports, and so forth. This shows professionalism and indicates to the reader that a serious effort to track the project is being made.
- If required, locate an outside evaluation team to be contracted to review the project and report progress; we recommend that an outside team be used on any very large project.
- Plan your project so that each activity is documented; the records can be used to evaluate the project.
- Organize the Evaluation Plan by goal; list the goal and then tell what evidence you will have that the goal has been accomplished.
- Include a discussion of the results you are looking for and how those results will be judged, both quantitatively and qualitatively.

## Continuation Plan—Introduction  1403.DOC

With few exceptions, funders want to fund lasting project that solve problems. The investment they are making is important. It is a seed planted to provide continuing benefit. If the project is clearly dependent on the requested funding and there is no way it will continue without it, it is unlikely it will be funded. On the bright side, however, if funding is provided for all the up-front set-up costs, then the funds to continue a given project are minimal by comparison. If your project solves a problem effectively, then it should not be too difficult to acquire support for its continuation.

Include the following in the Continuation Plan:

- Support for your project
- Detailed, reasonable action plans for acquiring financial support for your project before the termination of the funding being requested
- Details about any revenue that might be generated by the project
- Reference to letters of support (letters should actually appear in the Appendix) that may promise or imply future financial support if the project is successful.

## Continuation Plan—Example

The Business and Industry Association of Greater Granger has agreed to fund the maintenance contracts on all equipment necessary to continue this project. Please refer to the Letter of Support from the Association President in the Appendix on page 43. Key staff people will be absorbed in the District personnel budget over the five year grant period, at the rate of one staff person per year. The District is phasing out the XYZ program and, as a result, beginning in 1999, it will have slots that can be filled with project staff. Please refer to the statement by the District Superintendent in the Appendix on page 47. A small supplies and materials budget will be carved from budgets at the various schools served by the project. These commitments cover base costs to continue operation of the project.

To allow for growth and the acquisition of new equipment and materials, additional revenue will be necessary. Our students will be trained in graphic arts, so we intend to bid for District graphics projects, which in the past have gone to outside vendors. Projects such as the design and development of graphics, newsletters, District reports, and so forth will be sought on a competitive bid basis by the Project Coordinator. Revenue from this work will be set aside to cover new equipment and material needs for the project.

If the project succeeds as we predict it will, four other District Superintendents are interested in providing some funding for our project in return for consultative assistance in setting up a similar project in their schools. See letters of inquiry from two of these Superintendents in the Appendix on pages 50 and 51.

Our Parent Teacher Associations have agreed to assign 10 percent of the proceeds from their three major fundraisers to future support for the project once grant funding has ended. These funds will likely be earmarked for supplies since the funds for supplies from the schools (see paragraph one) will be minimal at best.

### *Tips for Creating a Good Continuation Plan*

- Make a solid, plausible case.
- Include a Continuation Plan even if the funder does not require one.
- Get letters of support, indicating future financial support.
- Refer to precedents in which your organization has continued projects beyond its original funding, thus showing a positive track record.
- Do not state that you will seek funding from other foundations of federal grant programs—that kind of statement does not show project independence!

## *Management Plan—Introduction*  1404.DOC

It is important for a prospective funder to be confident that your project will be administered effectively. One of the most common errors made by novice proposal writers is to forget that the project itself must be managed. It is not enough to have a great project—your organization must be capable of handling that project.

The Management Plan does not need to be complicated. In most cases, the manner in which the various components of the project will be handled is explained in other parts of the proposal. Unless otherwise directed by the funder, include a separate section summarizing the management plans for the project. This is done to ensure that the reader recognizes that you understand the management planning necessary to implement your project successfully. Of particular interest to the funder are the credentials of the project leaders.

Include the following in the Management Plan:

- Discussion of the major responsibilities of key personnel
- Discussion of the involvement and responsibilities of any "donated" and volunteer personnel
- Statement of how the fiscal management will be carried out
- Statement that the project will be evaluated in a professional manner (a full evaluation plan is needed for most projects, so details will be included in that section of the proposal)

- Statement that the project will be documented and how that documentation will be archived

## *Management Plan—Example*

The Crash School of Driving (CSD) will administer the proposed project under the Department of Vehicle Safety. The Department Head will be the direct supervisor of a full-time Project Coordinator. The Project Coordinator will schedule and supervise three certified safety instructors. Fiscal accountability will be the responsibility of the Vice President for Financial Affairs, who will submit records for review by state, federal, and local auditors pursuant to requirements by the grantor.

The Counseling Division will provide counselors for students participating in the project. Project reports, transcriptions of counseling sessions, and enrollment records will be the responsibility of the Project Coordinator and will be kept on file in the Administrative Office Building, Room B-12. Clerical support will be provided through the Administrative Secretarial Support Division. See Appendix D-1 for the Project Organizational Chart and Appendix D-2 for the Project Information Flow Chart.

Within the first Project Month (PM) the Department Head for Vehicle Safety will facilitate and implement a meeting with the Project Advisory Council, consisting of members of the vehicle safety community including City Police, County Police, Volunteer Emergency Service Council, City and County Fire Departments, and Hospital Safety staff (see listing in Appendix E-2). This Advisory Council will formulate plans and submit recommendations for implementation of project guidelines to the Project Coordinator.

During PMs 2 and PM 3, the Project Coordinator will test applicants and record results. After all applicants are tested, the Project Coordinator will submit a Report of Findings to the grantor for review and revision. After revisions are received, the Project Coordinator will then implement the Phase One Objectives, with guidance from the Department Head for Vehicle Safety. At the end of Phase One, an Advisory Committee meeting will be coordinated and led by the Project Coordinator to identify the specific courses to be added to the curriculum. A report will be generated and filed in the CSD Administrative Offices.

At the end of PM 3, the first payment is due from the grantor. The Vice President for Financial Affairs will prepare forms 1032 and 1033 for submission. Upon receipt of funds, they will be disbursed according to the approved formula.

During PMs 4 and 5, the Project Coordinator will advertise and interview applicants for the three instructional positions detailed in the Project Description. The most qualified applicants will be brought before the Advisory Committee for interview. The top three will be selected by vote of the Advisory Committee and hired by CSD according to Federal and State employment guidelines.

The Project Coordinator will provide full-time supervision of the project and will report progress bimonthly. During PMs 16 and 17, a comprehensive evaluation will be done by the Advisory Committee. The evaluation report will be available by the first week in PM 18.

### Tips for Creating a Good Management Plan

- Be brief and concise, while clearly showing that your project has a well-thought-out management plan of its own.
- Include an organization chart of your project; show where your project fits into the management of your organization.
- Include a flowchart illustrating project events or process.
- Include a flowchart illustrating the lines of communication.

# Time Lines—Introduction  1405.DOC

Your project should be planned out thoroughly enough to assign time frames to the major activities involved in setting up, implementing, and evaluating it. Time lines can be drawn using a computer graphics program or developed using a specialized graphing or charting program. Include the following in the Time Lines:

- Goals and objectives, with the start date and completion date; specific dates may not be possible since the start of a project may be dependent on grant funding and you might not know exactly when the money will be available; in this case, use project months or weeks (i.e., "project month 3" or "week 4 of the project")—we are calling these project months or weeks, "time frames."
- Time frames for major project milestones or special events
- Time frames of major reports or evaluations
- Time frames of important deadlines
- Time frames for special requirements of the funder such as audits, on-site visits, or studies

# Time Lines—Examples

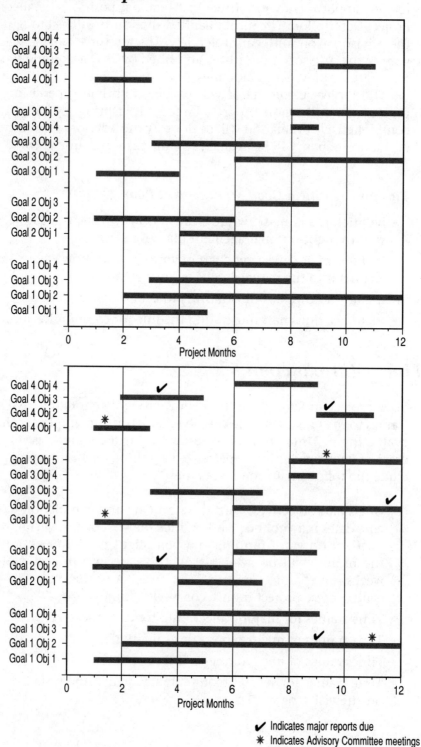

✔ Indicates major reports due
✳ Indicates Advisory Committee meetings

# Time Tables—Examples

Project Months

| | Start Month | Stop Month |
|---|---|---|
| Goal 1 Obj 1 | 1 | 5 |
| Goal 1 Obj 2 | 2 | 12 |
| Goal 1 Obj 3 | 3 | 8 |
| Goal 1 Obj 4 | 4 | 9 |
| Goal 2 Obj 1 | 4 | 7 |
| Goal 2 Obj 2 | 1 | 6 |
| Goal 2 Obj 3 | 6 | 9 |
| Goal 3 Obj 5 | 1 | 4 |
| Goal 3 Obj 4 | 6 | 12 |
| Goal 3 Obj 3 | 3 | 7 |
| Goal 3 Obj 2 | 8 | 9 |
| Goal 3 Obj 1 | 8 | 12 |
| Goal 4 Obj 4 | 1 | 3 |
| Goal 4 Obj 3 | 9 | 11 |
| Goal 4 Obj 2 | 2 | 5 |
| Goal 4 Obj 1 | 6 | 9 |

Project Months

| | Start Month | Stop Month | Reports | Advisory Mtgs |
|---|---|---|---|---|
| Goal 1 Obj 1 | 1 | 5 | 4 | |
| Goal 1 Obj 2 | 2 | 12 | | 2 |
| Goal 1 Obj 3 | 3 | 8 | 5 | |
| Goal 1 Obj 4 | 4 | 9 | | |
| Goal 2 Obj 1 | 4 | 7 | 7 | 4 |
| Goal 2 Obj 2 | 1 | 6 | | |
| Goal 2 Obj 3 | 6 | 9 | | 8 |
| Goal 3 Obj 5 | 1 | 4 | 4 | 1 |
| Goal 3 Obj 4 | 6 | 12 | | |
| Goal 3 Obj 3 | 3 | 7 | | |
| Goal 3 Obj 2 | 8 | 9 | | |
| Goal 3 Obj 1 | 8 | 12 | | |
| Goal 4 Obj 4 | 1 | 3 | 3 | 1 |
| Goal 4 Obj 3 | 9 | 11 | 11 | |
| Goal 4 Obj 2 | 2 | 5 | | |
| Goal 4 Obj 1 | 6 | 9 | | |

## Tips for Creating Good Time Lines

- Keep it simple; be sure your charts can be easily understood at first glance.
- Be sure your time frames are realistic—most people underestimate the time it takes to do things.
- Match the time frames to what has been said in the body of your proposal.
- Be sure the time line chart will reproduce when copied.

## Key Personnel—Introduction  1406.DOC

Funders want to know who will lead a project and what their qualifications are. They recognize that a project can be planned effectively, but if the people implementing the project are not qualified, the project can fail. It is important to take this part of the proposal seriously. It is important to tailor biosketches specifically to the project. Even though a project may not be funded until several months after you submit an application, most funders will want biosketches on real people. This may seem unrealistic because the people you submit may have other jobs by the time your grant is awarded. If the person whose biosketch you submit is no longer available when you receive the award, find another equally qualified person and notify your funder of the change in personnel. Get the funder's approval for the change. In some cases a funder recognizes the problem caused by a time lag from submission to notification and will allow you to submit a "qualifications" profile stating the requirements for the job. Examples of a biosketch and a qualifications profile have been provided.

Include the following in a Key Personnel Biosketch:

- Name and title or job function
- Position he or she will hold in the project
- Summary of skills in relation to the project
- Summary of specialties in relation to the project
- Experience relevant to the project
- Education (degrees, majors, minors)
- Awards or publications that indicate credentials valuable to the project

### Tips for Creating a Good Key Personnel Biosketch

- Do not simply submit a job history.
- Do not include unrelated credentials.
- Focus on qualifications to perform the job.
- Keep to one page unless directed otherwise.
- Interview the person to get appropriate information.
- Do not wait until the last minute to do biosketches.

# *Key Personnel—Example*

[Biosketch Type]

**John Doe, PhD, CDP, CPIM**
Department Head, Information Technology
Project Position: Program Coordinator
Project: Information Technology Systems Installation

## Specialties:
Project Management
System Analysis
Instructional Development

## Summary:
Dr. Doe has over thirty years of experience in project management related to institutional development and technical assessment and development. He has a background in computer systems analysis, information management and networking, educational management and forecasting, and account systems analysis. He has effectively planned and led implementation of three successful initiatives which were a part of large federal and state grants awards.

## Experience includes:
responsibility for feasibility study and strategic planning of data collection and processing capabilities in administrative applications for a large post-secondary education institution; implementation liaison for management information systems in a statewide effort funded through a grant from the National Technology Foundation; identification and training of faculty in use of management information systems; design, installation, and implementation of a class scheduling system for a medium size school district, achieving reduction in errors and significantly improving on-time information delivery to students and teachers; developing software products and implementing bar code data collection, enhancing user capabilities for a variety of computer systems to upgrade the state library system on a state grant; analysis and development of the strategic plan for the data collection system of a major university.

## Professional Activities:
Information Management Teachers Institute, Ohio University, Athens;
  Established and Organized Institute
AIM, Inc. (Automatic Identification Manufacturers), Chairman, Education
  Committee
Scan-Tech '88, '89, '90, Moderator

## Education:
Fordham University, BA, History
St. Louis University, MA, Industrial Engineering
George Washington University, PhD, Engineering Education

# Key Personnel—Example, continued

[Job Description Type]

## Project Director

### Education and Skill Requirements:

- Master's degree in administration, education, or social work
- Excellent communication skills
- Experience with large and small group presentations
- Strong organizational skills
- Experience with Federal regulation compliance and paperwork

**Reports to:** Director of Institutional Advancement

**Responsibilities:**
Perform all tasks necessary to ensure efficient and effective project management, including but not limited to the following:

- Scheduling and coordination of the following: orientation for mentors and staff, workshops, tours, tour debriefings, child care, transportation, and coursework
- Identifying, contacting, recruiting, and maintaining cooperative relationships with the following: area business and industry, community organizations, county and state agencies, and regional and national dissemination networks
- Developing promotional materials and making presentations to gain support for project continuation
- Developing a formalized project implementation plan for dissemination.
- Supervision and assistance of the Project Counselor

# Chapter 15

# Phase 3: The Budget and the Budget Justification

## *Introduction*

This chapter contains directions for creating two of the 18 pieces of the grant proposal, the Budget and the Budget Justification. As illustrated by Exhibit 15.1, work on the Budget can begin as soon as the goals and objectives are laid out, either separately or concurrently with those in Phase 2.

## *Budget—Introduction*

 1501.DOC

A complete budget for the project must be developed. The disk exercises that accompany Chapter 11 should have helped you formulate most of your numbers, and a filled-in version of the total budget can be found in the Example Section. This budget must include all items that your organization will contribute to the support of the project. It is common to forget to account for time of supervisory personnel and support staff, postage, copying costs, telephone charges, and other such expenses. You will be asking a single funder for funding for a portion of the project budget. You must decide what things you will ask for in light of the guidelines provided by the funder. Most funders want to see the total project budget. A total project budget includes both what you and any partners are contributing and what support you are asking from the funder. All federal funders and some foundation funders provide you with a summary budget form. A blank copy of the most common federal budget form (SF-424) is included in this toolkit under the tab labeled Additional Tools.

**EXHIBIT 15.1**

## Proposal Work Flow

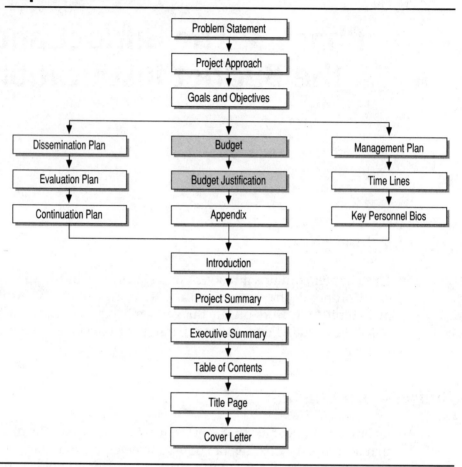

Include the following in the Budget:

- Personnel costs
- Personnel fringe costs
- Contractual costs
- Construction or renovation costs
- Materials
- Supplies
- Equipment
- Indirect costs (overhead)

- Travel costs
- In-kind contributions

### Terms That Can Cause Problems

***Personnel Benefits Costs.***   For every dollar that is paid to an employee, an employer incurs additional costs that can run as high as 45 cents per dollar. These additional costs are called "benefits" or sometimes "fringe benefits." What is this extra money and where does it go? The table in Exhibit 15.2 illustrates the various costs that go into benefits. Your individual situation may have more benefits costs or less. The actual types and amounts are determined locally.

In our example, for every $100.00 paid to an employee, the employer must spend $123.98.

Someone in your organization, probably in the Payroll Department, will have the amount of fringe figured as a percentage. Make sure you include the cost of fringe in your budget or the salary you anticipate being $20,000 will turn out to be $15,204 after the Payroll Department takes out its 23.98 percent. (Our example only—remember, your actual fringe will be different. You must check with your payroll department.)

***Indirect Costs.***   Costs that can be directly attributed to a project are called direct costs—for example, a project director's salary and fringe, the costs of operating a mobile diagnostic van, the costs of textbooks, or the costs of paper and pencils. The costs of these things can be easily figured, and it is plain that all the costs are directly because of the project.

### EXHIBIT 15.2

### Benefits: Type and Cost

| Description | Paid by Employer |
| --- | --- |
| FICA (Social Security and Medicare)* | 7.54% |
| SUTA State Unemployment* | 2.64% |
| FUTA Federal Unemployment | 0.8% |
| Workers' Compensation Insurance* | 1.5%[†] |
| Health Insurance** | 8.0% |
| Retirement Benefits** | 3.5% |
| TOTAL | 23.98% |

*Always paid by employer
**Sometimes paid by employer
[†]Amount will vary by occupation (very high for a logger, very low for a secretary)

A project also can incur other costs—for example, the electricity for lights; the maintenance and upkeep on a room; toilet paper, soap, and water used in the bathroom; the time it takes the Payroll Department to maintain records and generate the project director's checks and tax forms; and the share of the telephone used by the project personnel. All these things have some cost attached to them. Someone is paying for the electricity. Someone is paying to keep paper, soap, and running water in the bathrooms. Someone is paying for the Payroll Department to keep up with things. But how much of these costs can be attributed to your project? It is very hard to tell. These are known as indirect costs, sometimes called overhead.

The Financial Department of your organization has a percentage to use to figure indirect (overhead) costs.

***In-Kind.***   If your organization allocates the use of several computers to a project, then the purchase cost of the computers is an in-kind contribution of your organization to the project budget. If your organization allows an employee to work a quarter of his or her time on a project, then 25 percent of that person's salary and fringe are an in-kind contribution from your organization to the project budget.

In-kind contributions are noncash contributions made by you and/ or your partners. These in-kind contributions are assigned a fair and reasonable dollar value for inclusion in the total project budget. This puts a monetary amount to the involvement by you and your partner(s) in the project.

The following are a few typical items that organizations contribute on an in-kind basis:

- Employee time
- Full-time use of equipment
- Part-time use of equipment such as a copier (a percentage basis)
- Materials (books and software)
- Supplies
- Volunteer time (fair market value of donated time)
- Facilities (building space)
- Access to special support services such as technical consulting

*Caution*: You cannot use an item as an in-kind contribution then also claim the same item as an indirect cost. An item can only be claimed in one way, either as an in-kind contribution or as an indirect cost, but not both.

*Materials and Supplies.*   Supplies are consumables such as pencils and paper. Materials are also consumables, except that the time frame for consumption is much longer. Materials are things like books and software—things with a limited life span, but a much longer life than supplies.

Be sure to put all software purchases into the materials line item. Most funders want to keep the percentage of total budget spent on equipment to a minimum. One way to hold down the equipment line item is to move software into materials.

## Budget—Example

| Description | Requested Amount | Our Share | Partner Share | Project Total |
|---|---|---|---|---|
| **Personnel** | | | | |
| Project Director | 36,000 | | | 36,000 |
| Curriculum Supervisor | 12,000 | 12,000 | | 24,000 |
| Technology Supervisor | 12,000 | | 12,000 | 24,000 |
| **Personnel Fringe   35%** | | | | |
| Project Director | 12,600 | | | 12,600 |
| Curriculum Supervisor | | 4,200 | | 4,200 |
| Technology Supervisor | | | 4,200 | 4,200 |
| **Construction/Renovation** | | | | |
| Electrical & A/C | | 12,000 | | 12,000 |
| **Materials** | | | | |
| Software | 22,000 | 11,000 | | 33,000 |
| Textbooks | | 6,000 | | 6,000 |
| Video Tapes | | | 4,500 | 4,500 |
| Miscellaneous | 3,500 | | | 3,500 |
| **Supplies** | | | | |
| Classroom supplies | | 4,500 | | 4,500 |
| Computer supplies | 8,500 | | | 8,500 |
| **Equipment** | | | | |
| Computers | 45,000 | 25,000 | | 70,000 |
| Printers | 5,000 | 2,500 | | 7,500 |
| Modems | 1,200 | 1,200 | | 2,400 |
| **Travel** | | | | |
| Air Fare | 1,200 | | | 1,200 |
| Mileage | 750 | | | 750 |
| Lodging | 600 | | | 600 |
| Meals | 350 | | | 350 |
| **Contractual Services** | | | | |
| Childcare | | | 25,000 | 25,000 |
| Printing | | | 8,000 | 8,000 |

*(continued)*

## Budget—Example, continued

| Description | Requested Amount | Our Share | Partner Share | Project Total |
|---|---|---|---|---|
| Training | | | | |
| Registration & Materials | 2,000 | | | 2,000 |
| Stipends | 1,000 | | | 1,000 |
| Other | | | | |
| Outside Evaluation | 2,000 | | | 2,000 |
| Subtotal | 165,700 | 78,400 | 53,700 | 297,800 |
| Indirect Costs   8.5% | 14,085 | | | |
| Totals | 179,785 | 78,400 | 53,700 | 311,885 |

### Tips for Creating a Good Budget

- As you are developing your project, assign costs to everything.
- Be realistic.
- Carefully read directions from the funder regarding budgets.
- Use computer spreadsheets to help you tally costs.
- Be very thorough—the costs you forget will have to be absorbed by your organization.
- Do not make up figures—check costs and get bids.
- If you have any questions about the budget, call the program contact people; they are there to help you.

## Budget Justification—Introduction

The budget you provide the funder is a summary budget with line item totals only. In the summary budget, supplies, for example, will have just one figure, a total. In the Budget Justification, the reader is told where you got the totals you put in the budget summary. For example, suppose you allocated $1,000 for supplies. In the Budget Justification, you would show that $300 is for copy paper, $500 is for computer paper, and $200 is for computer ribbons. The Budget Justification is just what its name says: a "justification." In the Budget Justification, make a case that all items you are requesting are necessary and realistic. The Budget Justification is focused on the items being requested from the funder, but it is also a good idea to show your contribution to the project as well.

Include the following in a Budget Justification:

- The rationale for each item you request
- "Formulas" indicating where you got the totals recorded in the budget summary page(s)
- Persuasive statements indicating the need for major items being requested
- Items that match the Budget Summary and the proposal itself

## Budget Justification—Example

*Personnel.*   Three persons are required to perform the tasks outlined in the Goals and Objectives section of this proposal: (1) a *Project Coordinator*, Master of Science and Nursing—responsible for overall project planning, scheduling, supervision, administration and implementation, (2) a *Project Assistant*, Registered Nurse—responsible for assisting with screenings, education programs, driving the van, planning and scheduling education sessions, and, (3) a *Clerk/Secretary*—responsible for data entry, keeping records and files, and normal secretarial duties such as writing letters and setting referral appointments for clients. These three positions are necessary to carry out Goal II, Goal III, Goal IV, and Goal V. (Goals are stated on pages 35–37.)

*Equipment—Medical Van.*   The van itself meets specifications that are identical to the operating prototype at St. Joseph's Hospital in Tampa, Florida. Following the Year 1 budget is a copy of the brochure for the vehicle. The brochure lists these specifications and shows a diagram of the vehicle. None of the Goals of the project can be accomplished without the van. The cost of the van is $138,000.

**Equipment for Van**

| | | |
|---|---|---|
| 1. | PFT Spirometrix/Spiromate—SP2500 | $3,950 |
| 2. | Abbott Vision (cholesterol, glucose, hemoglobin) | 11,250 |
| 3. | Miles Seralyzem III (blood tests) | 5,000 |
| 4. | Accucheck (glucose) | 200 |
| 5. | Hematocrit (centrifuge & reader) | 1,500 |
| 6. | Stethoscope (5 each) | 100 |
| 7. | Auto BP (Blood Pressure) | 3,400 |
| 8. | Calculate BEE with Compu-Cal (basal energy expenditures) | 300 |
| 9. | Scales | 100 |
| 10. | Height tape | 30 |

*(continued)*

**Equipment for Van (*continued*)**

| | | |
|---|---|---:|
| 11. | Medical calipers | 225 |
| 12. | Microscope | 900 |
| 13. | Computer | 3,500 |
| 14. | Printer | 500 |
| 15. | Microwave | 200 |
| 16. | Refrigerator | 400 |
| 17. | Stove | 300 |
| 18. | Utensils | 100 |
| 19. | VCR and monitor | 800 |
| 20. | Cellular phone | 1,000 |
| 21. | Burglar alarm system | 500 |

The first 12 items are *testing and screening devices* to accomplish Goal II. The *computer and printer* will be used to gather data on the screenings and educational programs, for evaluation information, for communicating information to appropriate referral agencies and professionals, and for effective reporting and administration. The computer equipment helps accomplish Goal II, Goal III, and Goal V.

The *VCR and monitor* will be used to show educational video tapes to help accomplish Goal III. This equipment will allow the project staff to provide health care information to large groups of people in the communities served by the Wellness on Wheels project.

The *microwave, refrigerator, stove and cooking utensils* will be used for hands-on workshops on how to prepare nutritional meals and meals required by special diets (diabetic, low fat, low salt, etc.).

The *cellular phone* will be used to alert emergency medical services, physicians and others in case of injury or medical emergency. The van will be traveling to remote areas where there may not be an available telephone.

Due to the large amount of equipment on the van, the rural location of our facility, and the sites to which the van will be traveling, a *burglar alarm system* is a necessity.

***Supplies and Materials.*** *Note*: The amount requested in the budget is *not* the total amount needed to cover supplies. Because the customization of the van and installation of equipment will take a minimum of seven months, the first month of operation for the van will be Project Month (PM) 8. Therefore, in the budget for Project Year 1, only one quarter's supplies and materials are needed.

*Supplies for the screenings* (Goal II) include: alcohol, alcohol pads, Band-Aids, cleaning agents, disposable gloves, exam gowns, exam table covers, gauze pads, glass slides, lancets, peroxide, pipettes, reagents, serums, scissors, specimen cups, tape, thermometer, tissues, and other such items. Office supplies include pens, pencils, paper, computer disks, printer paper, are necessary to fulfill Goal V and to provide support for screenings and educational programs.

Publicity to notify communities about van schedules and programs will require *materials* including paper, poster board, printing, postage and long distance telephone access. These materials are used for Goal IV.

**Contractual.** Contractual arrangements include two items: (1) fee for performance of outside evaluations, $2,000, Goal V; and (2) extended warranty on the Abbot Vision equipment, $750, Goal II. Goals are on pages 35–37.

**Travel.** Travel costs include: three yearly trips by the project director to the annual DHHS CHC Project Director's Seminar in Washington, D.C. (as required by the funder) for a total of $4,500; and three yearly trips by the project director to the Rural Hospital Association State Convocation in Atlanta (as required by the funder) for a total of $1,500.

**Training.** Yearly recertification training as required by the Certification Board of CHC for all caregiving staff will cost $15,000 over the three years of the project.

### Tips for Creating a Good Budget Justification

- Keep in mind that your goal is for the reader to think, "Of course they need that for this project."
- The Budget Justification should be brief and concise.
- "Cut and paste" charts from computer spreadsheets used to develop the budget.
- The Budget Justification can be written in bullets and phrases.
- Relate each request for a major item to the Goal that item supports.

# Chapter 16

# Phase 4: Appendix

## *Introduction*

A properly used Appendix contains information that expands and explains, in detail, points that are made in the body of a proposal. The material that goes into an Appendix is collected during the creation of all the other sections (see Exhibit 16.1).

## *Appendix—Introduction*

The Appendix contains supplementary materials to support the proposal. Most funders discuss what they want included in the Appendix. If there is no guidance from the funder, include only things that are absolutely necessary to support your proposal or things that will enhance it. The purpose of the Appendix is to handle material that, if included in the body of the proposal, would interrupt the flow of thought.

Include the following in an Appendix:

- Biographical sketches of key personnel
- Organization charts
- Time lines and charts
- Letters of support
- Survey results
- Equipment descriptions
- Lists of advisors and board members
- Descriptive information about your organization
- Statistical information

Exhibit 16.1

## Stage in Work Flow

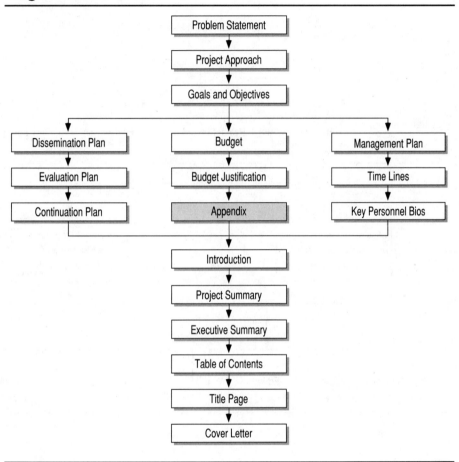

# Appendix Example—Project Organization Chart

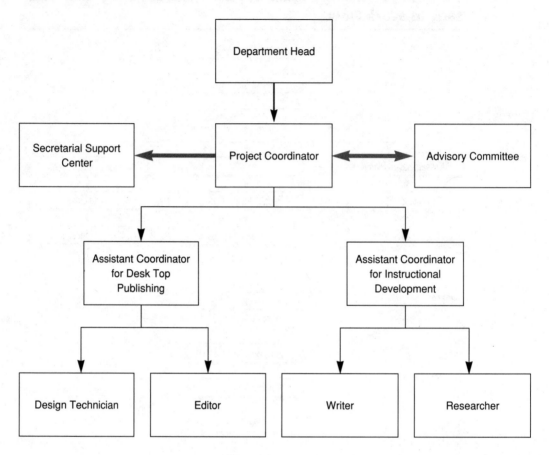

# Letter of Support

**TQN** Industries
2020 Horizon Road
Sunview, KS 40987

September 1, 1998

Dr. Joseph H. Bishop
Superintendent
Crowel County Schools
PO Box 3465
Lark, KS 40985

Dear Joseph:

It is with pleasure that I write this letter to you concerning our recent discussions about providing guest lecturers for your vocational classes. Eight of our staff have agreed to devote 5 hours each per month for that purpose. Three of those staff members are first line technicians working directly with Computer Aided Design in relation to blueprint development. Two of the staff are field engineers, and as such have the responsibility to translate the blueprints into finished product. The remaining three are supervisors and managers and can give students a view of the business aspects of the engineering and construction industry.

In addition, we are prepared to give your instructors copies of software we have developed in-house to perform design functions. Much of our software is highly sensitive and proprietary in nature, but there are some applications that are useful, but not "top secret." Our technicians will be glad to install the software and train your instructors.

As discussed, TQN is willing to donate $2,500 as matching funds for your grant proposal to the Institute of Current Technology. A check will be cut as soon as you are notified of award.

The project you are undertaking is highly valuable to your students and to the industrial community. Your graduates consistently rank at the top on productivity as employees. Please let me know if I can be of further assistance.

Sincerely,

Thomas Q. Nealey
President

TQN/jl

## Bibliography

Include the following in a Bibliography:

- Major references used in the proposal (books, articles, and other publications)
- Important studies backup up the need and project approach
- Internal studies backing up the need and project approach

### Tips for Creating a Good Bibliography

- All references must be recent (within the past year) unless the reference is a milestone document that is generally accepted as a landmark.
- Include only key references—a bibliography should be only one or two pages for most proposals.
- Be sure to include the funder's own publications if you referenced them.
- There are many acceptable formats for bibliographies.

### Example Bibliographic References

Horton-Hughes: passages from *Who's On First* by Solomon Breakstone and *Capital Expenditures* by G. Turner, J. Croft, and G.W. Stewart.

Thomas M. Thompkins: passage from "There is Soup on Your Tie" in *American News & Flash*, January 7, 1990.

Amos, Patrick T. *Teacher's Guide to Crime and Punishment*, San Francisco, CA: McGraw-Hill, 1989.

Barlow, Susan G. *Train Your Children*, St. Louis, MO: Apprentice-Hull, 1988.

F. Bellows, "Sensors, Controls, and Machinery," *New Wave Science*, vol. 233, no. 6655, August 1, 1989, pp. 1327–39.

A. Brank, *Play and Work*, TIM Press, Cambridge, Mass., 1990.

Carson SG: Combating the age barrier to learning, in Jones S, Gibson ML (eds): *Readings in Education*, Education Tomorrow publication no. 22–67. New York, National Institute on Learning Theory, 1990, pp. 55–102.

James, EE: *The Dynamics of Reading*. Juneau, MD, Prime Books, 1989.

## Endnotes

Unless directed otherwise, put all endnotes on a separate page in the Appendix. As with the Bibliography, there are many acceptable formats for footnotes.

### Endnotes

*Notes to Pages 99–113*

11. 37 C.F.R. Ch. II, 202.19.
12. Carson SG: Combating the age barrier to learning, in Jones S, Gibson ML (eds): *Readings in Education*, Education Tomorrow publication no. 22–67. New York, National Institute on Learning Theory, 1990, p. 56.
13. *Grandma Taylor Properties, Inc.* v. *This Month Magazine*, 117 F. Supp. 348; 7874-5 (daily ed. Sept. 22, 1976).
14. *Ibid.*

### Tips for Creating a Good Appendix

- When in doubt, cut—do not load up the Appendix with extraneous material.
- Put in significant enhancements only; if you do not refer to it in the body of the proposal, it doesn't belong in the Appendix.
- Regarding letters of support, do not include "attaboys" and "attagirls." Readers know it is easy to get most anyone to write a letter saying your organization is deserving of funding; these letters are disregarded for the most part. Funders want to see letters that establish genuine support for your project or that back up the need for the project.
- Do not cheat—strictly adhere to a funder's page limit.

# Chapter 17

# Phase 5: Introduction, Executive Summary, Table of Contents, Title Page, and Cover Letter

## *Introduction*

This section contains directions for five of the 18 stages of the final grant proposal writing process (see Exhibit 17.1). Although all of these components appear at the beginning of the finished proposal, they are not created first, but last.

## *Cover Letter—Introduction*  1701.DOC

Unless a funder indicates otherwise, always include a cover letter with your proposals. The cover letter does not count in the page limit requirement. The cover letter should not be attached or bound together with the proposal, but should be placed, loose, on top of the original copy of the proposal.

### *Why Send a Cover Letter?*

- To show your professionalism—submitting a proposal is a business transaction. The use of cover letters is standard business practice.
- To make a few key points, right up front. The cover letter is the first thing a reader may see, and it can set the tone for the whole proposal.
- To establish rapport with the reader.

## Exhibit 17.1

## Work Flow of Proposal

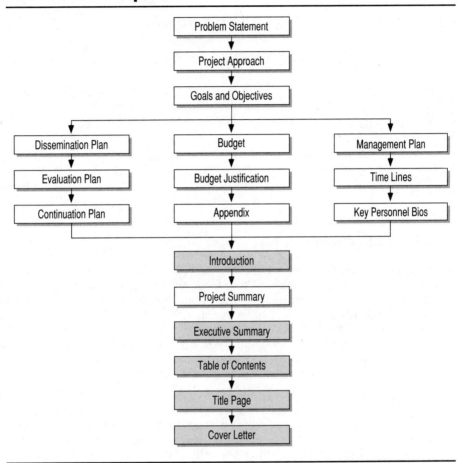

Include the following in a Cover Letter:

- An introduction to your organization—who and what you are
- Your purpose for submitting a proposal
- Statement of how your project fits with the grantor's program focus
- Persuasive statements about the merits of your project
- Appreciation for the opportunity to submit a proposal

# Cover Letter—Example

**District Schools**
8921 Shadey Lane
Middleburg • Georgia • 44444

July 15, 1999

Dr. Susan Perkins
Program Director
National Institute for Technology Planning
1790 Brook Glen Plaza
Washington, DC 20323

Dear Dr. Perkins:

Subject: Program Solicitation NITP 49.3265

Middleburg District Schools, Middleburg Georgia, is pleased to apply for funding in response to the above solicitation. Your focus on assistance to rural schools in a labor surplus area perfectly matches the profile of our community. We are located in the South central area of Georgia. Our service area, Cole County, is a federally designated labor surplus county. Previously a primarily agricultural area, industry is slowly taking over our farmland. Due to changes in the needs of our population, we must institute instructional programs to prepare our work force for vastly different careers. Our tax base is not increasing rapidly enough to fund the equipment we need to provide a relevant, quality curriculum.

Our proposed project is designed to upgrade our vocational curriculum and equipment while providing special counseling for students by area industry representatives. The community's commitment is compelling. To date, we have 37 letters of agreement to provide volunteer career counseling. Our request is for industrial maintenance equipment and funding for evaluation and analysis to develop a special curriculum to match the skill requirements of area industry. In addition, we need funding for special training for our instructors.

We are impressed with your progressiveness and response to the needs of the educational opportunities for our community while providing a model for other rural school districts.

If you have questions, please contact Sally Pearson, our Lead Teacher on this project. Her telephone number is 404-322-2222. Thank you.

Sincerely,


Carol C. Graham
Superintendent

CCG/gt
Enclosures

### *Tips for Creating a Good Cover Letter*

- Keep the letter to one page.
- Use a professional business letter format.
- Use a subject line.
- Left justify only; don't full justify. You want to make it easy on the reader, and the extra spaces inserted for full justification make reading more difficult.
- The letter should come from the highest manager involved in submitting your project (such as a district superintendent or hospital administrator); if this person is not the contact person for the project, name the contact person and provide his or her telephone number in the body of the letter.
- Proof and reproof; this letter is the very first thing a reader may see, if there is a misspelling or grammatical error, the reader's expectations about your ability and project will be significantly lowered.
- Use a text font at 12 points for a cover letter.

## *Title Page—Introduction*  1702.DOC

A title page is the "cover" of your proposal. If the proposal is bound, the title page should be printed on card stock. The whole purpose of a title page is to eliminate all possible confusion about what the document contains, who it is to, who it is from, and who the grantor should get in touch with if there are questions concerning the proposal or the project.

Include the following in a Title Page:

- Identification of the grantor's program by number of name
- For a proposal to the federal government, the transmittal deadline date (the date on which the proposal must be at the grantor agency)
- For a proposal to a foundation, the date of the review cycle for which the proposal is submitted (some foundation proposals are in response to a request for proposal—in that case, the submittal deadline is the date to use)
- Identification of the organization to which the proposal is being submitted
- The title of your project
- Identification of the organization that is submitting the proposal
- Contact person's name and telephone number

## Title Page—Examples

---

(Federal Government Proposal)

### Response to Solicitation Number NITP 49.3265

August 1, 1999

National Institute for Technology Planning

Special Projects Division
1790 Brook Glen Plaza
Washington, DC 32323

Attention: Dr. Susan Perkins, Director

Proposed Project

### New Century Vocational Readiness

Submitted by:

Middleburg Integrated School District
2020 Marsh Street
Middleburg, GA 40404

Contact:

Kathryn Gordon
555-111-2222

---

## *Title Page—Examples, continued*

(Foundation Proposal)

## **Grant Proposal**

### **Submitted to**

The Smith Family Foundation
123 Main Street
Home Town, TX 12345

for Consideration During the August 1999 Review Cycle

Attention: Ms. Susan Perkins



Proposed Project

## **New Century Vocational Readiness**



Submitted by:

Middleburg Integrated School District
2020 Marsh Street
Middleburg, GA 40404



Contact:

Kathryn Gordon
555-111-2222

### *Tips for Creating a Good Title Page*

- Be sure the address on the title page is the correct delivery address. This address may be different from the normal mailing address of a grantor.

- Eliminate all confusion as to where the proposal should go and from whom it came.

- Project titles should be clever but not cutesy. A project title with a clever twist or sound or acronym is easily remembered by a reader.

- Project titles should be descriptive but not wordy—five to seven words maximum.

- The person who is named on the title page should be the person who knows the most about the project and can answer any questions the grantor may have.

- Make arrangements so the contact person is available to take any telephone calls from the grantor—for example, make sure the school secretary knows about the proposal so the secretary understands the urgency of a call from the grantor.

# *Table of Contents—Introduction*  1703.DOC

A Table of Contents should be included in any proposal longer than five pages. A federal agency will always expect to see one. The purpose of a Table of Contents is to provide one place where a reader can quickly and easily find any particular part or section and be told the page on which that part or section starts.

Include the following in a Table of Contents:

- Section headings to all the major sections of the proposal
- Subsection headings to all important subsections contained in a major section
- All sections named by the grantor as belonging in the proposal
- Sequential page numbers on which each section or subsection begins

# *Table of Contents—Examples*

## Table of Contents—Examples, continued

(Foundation Proposal)

### Tips for Creating a Good Table of Contents

- Carefully follow any and all directions given by the grantor concerning such things as page numbering, forms, and order of sections.

- Always use the grantor's terminology. If the grantor asks for a Project Calendar rather than a Time Line, then call it a Calendar in the Table of Contents; if the grantor asks for a Project Abstract rather than a Project Summary, then call it a Project Abstract in the Table of Contents.

- Make the Table of Contents reader friendly. Readers frequently use the table of contents as a checklist to see that all required parts have been included in a proposal; do not make a reader search for a part.

- The Table of Contents should provide clear directions to all parts of a proposal. The operative word here is *all*—every significant part of a proposal must have its own entry in the Table of Contents.

- Include forms even if they are not page numbered.

- The Table of Contents is the last piece of a proposal to be completed. It must be created after all page numbering of the proposal is completely settled.

## Executive Summary—Introduction  1704.DOC

Federal proposals are usually highly prescribed with a cover form that contains most of the information one would include in an Executive Summary. It is likely, therefore, that an Executive Summary will not be required. Add an Executive Summary to the proposal if you can do so while adhering to page limits and the required organization of the proposal.

Foundations have guidelines, but most do not have a formalized request for proposal (RFP). It is a good idea to include an Executive Summary with every foundation proposal unless the foundation specifically says otherwise.

It is critical to include an Executive Summary with any proposal to a corporation. Often, the Executive Summary is the primary part of the document considered by busy executives.

Include the following in an Executive Summary:

- The project title
- The contact person for your project (the person who knows the most about the project) and his or her telephone number
- Your organization's official name and address

- A one-sentence statement of the problem your project addresses
- A mission statement for your project
- A very brief summary description of your project
- A two- or three-sentence description of the results you expect from the successful completion of your project

## Executive Summary—Example

***Project Title.***   Improving Writing Skills with Computer Communications

***Contact Person.***   Dr. James Harris, Department Head, English Department, 555-111-2222

***Proposal Submitted By.***   The Unified School District of Smith County, 1111 North Academy Street, Smith, California 90876

***Problem Statement.***   From ninth grade on, average progress in written language skills declines by as much as 20 percent a year through graduation. Our average high school graduate writes on an eighth-grade level.

***Mission Statement.***   By the end of the fourth year of the project, the average high school graduate will be able to write on an eleventh grade level.

***Project Synopsis.***   The target group for the project consists of approximately 800 ninth grade students in two high schools. Each student will have access to a computer terminal connected to a modem for one hour per day. During this hour, students will:

- Write letters to other students in 23 states and four foreign countries
- Maintain topical discussion sections on specially designed computer bulletin boards
- Design and lead "on-line" writing courses for students in other states
- Co-author research papers with students from other states using electronic mail

***Results.***   Students will be highly motivated to improve writing skills and will become at ease with writing concepts and structure. Since students in the test group will have four year's exposure to intensive work on writing skills, expectations are for a drastic improvement in writing skills as exhibited by improved writing skill test scores. Our target is for an improvement equivalent to four grade levels by the time the test group of students graduates from high school.

***The Request of XYZ Foundation.*** Our request is for $102,547 to purchase modems and software packages to make the on-line systems necessary to communicate with students in other states and countries and to implement electronic bulletin boards.

***Our Investment.*** Our school district has purchased over $1 million in technology to support this project. In addition, the Smith Community Foundation has contributed $350,000 in funding for supplementary texts and software as well as provided 23 volunteers to work with students. USA On-Line, Inc., is donating free time on its system so that our students can send mail and access databases for research. The local telephone company is donating line installation and hook-ups for the modems. We are seeking additional support from ABC Foundation, and through the EFG program offered by the U.S. Department of Education.

### Tips for Creating a Good Executive Summary

- Make a clear heading for each topic listed in the preceding (Example).
- Write in short, concise sentences.
- Use bulleted lists where possible rather than sentences.
- Concentrate on the essence of your project; do not try to explain all the ramifications and components in an Executive Summary.
- Normally, an Executive Summary should be no more than one page in length.

# Introduction—Introduction  1705.DOC

The Introduction lays the groundwork for the body of the proposal. Its proposal is to set the stage for the reader. Introductions should be brief, certainly no more than one page. Grantors will normally require that one of two parts begin the proposal narrative, either the Problem Statement or the Project Summary. The Introduction belongs at the beginning of whichever part begins the proposal narrative. In a long proposal, an Introduction may be up to a page in length. In a short proposal, an Introduction may be only a paragraph or two. Funders do not ask for an Introduction. It is up to you to include one at the beginning of your proposal. If an Introduction is not included, you will launch immediately into either the Problem Statement or Project Summary and the reader will not have been properly introduced to your organization, your locality, and your target population.

Include the following in an Introduction:

- A brief description of your organization, its size, makeup, and location

- A brief description of your service population and the type of community you serve. Relate your description to your project if possible (for example, if your project is focused on getting disadvantaged children into college, then your community profile might include a description of the general educational level of people in your community).

- Compare your organization and service community to other communities in your state and the nation. Use statistical comparisons when possible and appropriate.

- A one-sentence description of your project, whom it will serve, and what problem it solves.

- State up front how your project fits or matches the requirements and "hot buttons" of the funder.

- Explain what the results of your problem will be in an impact statement.

## Introduction—Example

The Brown County Consolidated School District, Brown County, Utah, is composed of 12 schools, including three high schools, three middle schools, and six primary schools. Two outreach programs are an integral part of our District efforts—our Adult Literacy program, offering eight classes per week, serving 100 adults in various community centers throughout the county; and our evening non-traditional school program, serving 68 students. This year our District is serving a total of 6,218 students and their families. Over 80 percent of our school population is white, with 15 percent Native Americans and 5 percent other minorities. We are located in Southeastern Utah in a large, mostly rural, sparsely populated county made up of small, independent communities with no large towns. Brownsville is the largest town, with a population of 25,000. The land area of the county is the second largest in the state.

The people we serve come primarily from farming, herding, and mining backgrounds. Most people in our community have not received a high school education. Only 32 percent of our population has completed high school, as compared to an average of 67 percent for the state and 73 percent for the nation. The low numbers of skilled laborers in our area contribute to a low level of industrial growth.

Our project, *That's Life: Life Skills for Teens*, is designed to broaden the horizons of our youth by teaching them skills necessary to set goals and make education and career decisions to improve their quality of life for the future. Though we are highly progressive in academic curriculum areas, winning the Utah Award for Excellence in Instruction, more than academics is necessary for our youth to successfully compete in the job market. We have held two life skills seminars in our area, one about job opportunities and requirements, and one about today's costs of living. These two programs were very well attended and received, but they were not enough. Topics must be expanded and offered to all students as a regular part of their educational process. As one of our students who attended the seminars put it, "I don't know the first thing about living anywhere but in Rocky Cove—there's a whole world out there I don't know how to live in. I don't even know what I need to know." Thirty-seven volunteers from state agencies, universities, businesses, and industries are ready to teach short courses for our project.

In *Today's Progress*, your company's annual report, it is stated that your focus is on improving the ability of young people to cope in today's environment. Our project perfectly meets your objective. It is focused on your people, ages 13 to 17, and is designed specifically to address basic life skills. All the citizens in our county have been involved in the design of this project through town meetings. Both potential participants and our citizens are excited about the project. We expect that participants will achieve the basic skills and confidence to cope independently with education, career, and day-to-day living. Evidence of the success of our program will include a six-year, long-range study of participants to follow their progress.

### Tips for Creating a Good Introduction

- Be concise; the Introduction should not describe everything about your organization and your project. It is simply a beginning or preface to your proposal.
- The Introduction is one place in the proposal where you can use a simple anecdote to illustrate the problem your project addresses.
- Be sure your Introduction follows a logical, cohesive sequence.
- Use the prospective funder's own words to introduce your project. (If the funder is looking for "a comprehensive, model program serving disadvantaged Hispanic preschoolers," clearly say, "Our XYZ project is a comprehensive program serving disadvantaged Hispanic preschoolers and is designed to be a model for other schools to follow."

Do not assume that readers will "read between the lines" and figure out on their own that your project fits the funder's profile.)

- Sometimes a funder has an "extra credit" option such as "special attention will be paid to those organizations serving 40 percent or more minority populations;" you are not required to meet the option, but are put in a special category if you do. When you fit a special category, state it clearly: "Our organization serves more than 50 percent minorities."

# Chapter 18

# The Final Proposal Package and Conclusion

## *The Final Package*

For the grantseeker, the hard work is now done. All that remains is to construct the project, which, after all the research, project definition, and numbers crunching, will seem like the easy part. First, the grantseeker should make one last pass of the project, to make sure that it is a complete project that responds to a problem, not a symptom; that the project is a good match for the grantor; that the hot buttons have been determined; that the budgets have been established and itemized; and that the plan is complete (see Exhibit 18.1).

Second, the grantseeker will want to make sure that all the publishing requirements have been met. Essentially, make sure that all the pages are facing forward, the pages have been numbered, the pages are clean and clear, copies have been made, signatures are where they should be, and a title page has been placed on the front. Determined if the grantor will want a proposal that is bound or unbound, and prepare the proposal accordingly (see Exhibit 18.2).

Finally, the moment the grantseeker has been waiting for—the proposal is ready to go in the mail. The grantseeker's first duty will be to stand back and admire it for a moment, but only for a moment. Ensure that copies of the proposal have been archived, a box or envelope that will fit the entire proposal has been found, and efforts have been made to ensure that the proposal will safely arrive by its appointed delivery date (see Exhibit 18.3).

EXHIBIT **18.1**                                                                1801.DOC

## Proposal Checklist

### Page 1 of 3

Proposed Project _____

Funder _____

❏   The guidelines from the targeted funder have been received and all necessary research on the funder has been completed (refer to the Funding Source Research Toolkit).

❏   A thorough outline of the funder's requirements for the proposal content has been written and double-checked by a second person.

❏   A thorough outline of the funder's requirements for publishing the proposal has been written and double-checked by a second person.

❏   A thorough outline of the potential sales points (hot buttons) has been written based on information about the funder gained from your research and from the RFP or guidelines.

❏   Research to support your problem statement has been completed.

❏   Research to support your proposed methodology (approach) has been completed.

❏   Research to support the expected results on successful completion of your project has been completed.

❏   Biosketches have been done on all key personnel.

❏   Appropriate letters of support have been acquired.

❏   Partnership arrangements have been made and documented of involvement of partners has been acquired.

❏   Supplementary documentation required by the funder has been obtained (tax status letter, annual report, annual budget summary, etc.).

❏   The budget for the entire project has been developed and you have the summary figures as well as a complete itemization.

❏   You have a list of the items in the overall budget that are being requested from the funder, the items being supplied by your organization, and what items are being supplied by other organizations.

❏   You know why each item in the budget is being requested so you can write solid budget justification.

**EXHIBIT 18.1** *Continued*

## Proposal Checklist

## Page 2 of 3

Proposed Project_____

Funder _____

- ❏ The project is thoroughly developed (refer to the Project Development Toolkit)
- ❏ The Problem Statement is written.
- ❏ The Project Approach is written.
- ❏ Goals and Objectives are written.
- ❏ The Dissemination Plan is written.
- ❏ The Evaluation Plan is written.
- ❏ The Continuation Plan is written.
- ❏ The Management Plan is written.
- ❏ Time Lines are drawn.
- ❏ Key Personnel Bios are written.
- ❏ The Budget is written.
- ❏ The Budget Justification is written.
- ❏ The Introduction is written.
- ❏ The Project Summary is written.
- ❏ The Executive Summary is written.

**E**XHIBIT **18.1** *Continued*

## Proposal Checklist

## Page 3 of 3

Proposed Project_____

Funder _____

- ❏ The Appendix is put together.
- ❏ The Table of Contents is written.
- ❏ The title page is created.
- ❏ The cover letter is written.
- ❏ Drafts of all sections of the proposal have been reviewed for content.
- ❏ According to content review, revisions have been made.
- ❏ The proposal is formatted according to the guidelines set by the funder.
- ❏ A draft of the entire proposal is proofed for grammar, spelling, format and "look" by at least two people.
- ❏ Corrections have been made to the proposal based on proofing suggestions.
- ❏ All forms have been completed and appropriate signature(s) obtained.
- ❏ The cover letter is written and appropriate signature(s) obtained.
- ❏ A master original of the entire proposal is printed, forms have been integrated into the proposal in appropriate places, and supplementary material included.
- ❏ The master original is checked against the funder's requirements.
- ❏ A Table of Contents is developed and proofed.
- ❏ Use the publishing and packaging checklists in Section Nine to complete the process.

## EXHIBIT **18.2**

 1802.DOC

## Publishing Checklist

Proposed Project_____

Funder _____

❏ Proposal is in the format required by the funder (page numbers, margins, type size, etc.) and has been laser printed

❏ Every page is clean and clear (no spots or smudges, no "white-out," all text centered on page, and graphics and charts are clear)

❏ No section of the proposal exceeds page limits set by the funder

❏ All forms are completed, including appropriate signatures (include all forms even if not filled out—write a big N/A on forms that aren't filled out)

❏ The pages of the proposal, including forms, are in the order required by the funder

❏ The Table of Contents has been done and includes all sections required by the funder, all important subsections, all forms, and is easy to follow—page numbers correspond exactly to the proposal

❏ A title page has been made that includes at least the following information: the solicitation number or title of the grant for which you are applying; the contact person, address and telephone number of the organization to which you are applying; the deadline date; the number of the project; and your contact person, organization name, address and telephone number

❏ The appropriate number of copies of the original have been made—remember that your organization will need copies

❏ Binding has been done according to either the requirements of the funder or professional business standards.

❏ If documents are not supposed to be bound, both the copies and the original to be sent to the funder have been "packaged" according to requirements

❏ Each copy of the proposal has been reviewed page by page—each copy has all the required pages, all pages are in the correct order, and all pages are printed correctly

❏ A nonbound hard copy of the entire proposal, including forms is securely archived along with a computer disk copy

EXHIBIT **18.3**

 1803.DOC

## Packaging and Posting Checklist

Proposed Project_____

Funder _____

❏ I have a box or envelope the right size to hold the original and all required copies of the proposal without wrinkling the pages and that is heavy enough to avoid shipping damage

❏ If copies are not to be bound, I have a blank envelope for each copy so that copies can be separated, or I have a "separator page" to place between each copy so the recipient can easily separate copies

❏ I have a typed shipping label with the correct address

❏ I am shipping with enough lead time to allow me to trace a lost shipment, make new copies and re-ship to meet the funder's deadline

❏ I am shipping with a carrier that guarantees delivery in the time frame required and one that provides a receipt—the carrier I am using can easily trace my package if necessary

❏ The appropriate number of copies have been made, including those required by the funder and the copies needed for our organization.

❏ A nonbound hard copy of the entire proposal, including forms has been securely archived along with a computer disk copy.

❏ Binding has been done according to either the requirements of the funder or professional business standards

❏ The box (envelope) has been sealed securely and the label affixed according to the carrier's requirements

❏ Shipping is completed on _____ (date and time)

❏ The air bill or receipt number for the package is _____

❏ According to the follow-up telephone call with carrier, the proposal package was received at (date and time) _____ and signed for by _____

# *Four Philosophies/Concepts*

So concludes the detailed overview of the grantseeking process. This volume covered the process of seeking a grant and asking for a grant. The process started with defining a problem or need. Remember that in grantseeking, a problem and a need are the same thing. The next step was to develop a project to solve the problem, as grantseeking projects are solutions to problems. Next, the potential funding sources to finance your solution were found. Finally, a proposal to directly ask for grant funding was developed.

In spite of how long and complex this book may seem, it has covered, and very rapidly, only one of the three major topics in the overall field of grants. The topic covered was strictly grantseeking. The methods on how to set up a grantseeking process within an organization were not discussed. Of the hundreds of questions that need to be answered in the setting up of a grantseeking effort within an organization, here are just a few: What skills are needed to be successful? What personnel should be involved? How are decisions made about which grants to pursue and which to leave alone? How does one keep the tail from wagging the dog, from letting the pursuit of grants drive the mission and purpose of the organization?

Also, the methods to run the project once an organization gets the grant were not examined. Much of the success in getting more grants hinges on how well an organization runs the project funded by the first grant it gets. Again, of the many questions that need to be answered about this topic, here are a few: How should the grant funds be handled from a financial perspective? How should personnel financed by the grant be managed? How should a grantee communicate with a grantor? How is the project evaluation handled? How is a grant project sustained after funding runs out? How is information disseminated about the project?

Let's get away from what is not covered in this book and back to the subjects that are covered. There are four key guiding philosophical concepts that are implicit throughout this volume, and that serve as a foundation to grantseeking. These are not the only philosophies necessary to successful grantseeking; however, these four serve as a good foundation, and could be termed "The Keys to the Kingdom."

*Concept One*: Grantseeking is a process not an event. This is the first of the four "keys to the kingdom." The problem that this philosophy helps to address is that even good grant seekers will fail more often than they succeed. Remember that the grants being sought are competitive project grants, not formula, not "wired," not straight applications. This is funding for which organizations compete against the lots of other organizations and funding that is awarded to only a few.

How then does one succeed at a task at which one will fail more often than succeed? The answer is to attempt the task repeatedly, over and over, again and again; ask anyone in door-to-door sales. If the organization pursues a grant on a one-time basis, an event, the chances are it will fail. If, however, one pursues grants repeatedly, submitting proposals regularly, then you will win your share and you will be successful. Good grantseekers will win 30 to 40 percent of the proposals they submit.

*Concept Two*: Attack problems, not symptoms. This philosophy will help one to develop projects that have a reasonable chance of success. Symptoms are seen on the surface. Problems are the things that cause the symptoms. For a project to be effective, it must work on one or more underlying problems that are causing a symptom; Attacking symptoms can be satisfying but will not be ultimately successful. Also, giving an example is dangerous business, because feelings run wide and deep about most problems, and no matter what example is chosen, someone will disagree. So rather than use a grant project example, consider let's talk about the flu. One symptom of the flu can be fever. Will treating the fever cure the flu? No, it will not. The symptoms of fever are often treated, because running too high a fever for too long can create problems of its own, but treating the fever will not cure the flu. If the cause of the fever is ignored and the high temperature is treated, there is the risk that the success at our project—getting the fever down—will still result in having the patient die, because the virus that is attacking the body was not treated. Successful grant projects attack problems not symptoms.

*Concept Three*: Make the match. This is the third key to the kingdom, and it refers to picking the best funding sources. One way to nudge the success rate higher is to submit only to funding sources from which one has an excellent possibility of getting funding, for which one makes the exact match. The random approach in grantseeking is a waste of time, both for the grantseeker and the grantor. There are a number of things the grantseeker should be sure of before they contact a grantor: that the grantor funds your type of organization; that the grantor funds their type of project; is interested in the same problems they are; that the grantor funds the type of things the grantseeker wants to purchase, such as personnel, equipment, travel, or all the rest; that the grantor makes grants in the range of the grantseeker's budget amount; that the grantor funds organizations in the grantseeker's geographic area and with their demographics; and that grant funds will be available when they are needed. The grantseeker should line up all aspects of their organization with those of the grantor. In short, make the match.

*Concept Four*: Remember the reader. The federal government does not read the proposal. A state government does not read the proposal. A foundation does not read the proposal. A person reads the proposal. When writing a proposal, indeed when writing anything, remember the audience. Who are the readers of grant proposals? To paraphrase Walt Kelley's Pogo, "We have met the reader and the reader is us." Yes the readers are just like you. That person will have all the typical adult problems, things such as an aching back, a flat tire, lost luggage, and a teenage child with green hair. If a proposal bores you, the grantseeker, it will bore that reader. If you, as a grantseeker, don't enjoy reading the proposal, neither will that reader. The simplest way to overcome this problem is to bring in an outside, uninterested, uninvolved reader. Be very careful. When an outside reader is used, and that person does not understand something in the proposal, it is not the reader's fault. It is the grantseeker's. It is the proposal that is at fault. An average person of average intelligence should be able to read your proposal and understand your problem and your solution.

## The Rules

What else remains to be said in conclusion? How about "the rules." Everyone likes a list of rules. It all seems so simple and orderly. Just keep firmly in mind that rules always oversimplify a messy, complex situation into what appears to be orderly, defined process. With that warning in mind, here are the "rules."

1. Read instructions thoroughly, completely, and painstakingly.
2. Follow instructions absolutely.
3. Call, email, or fax the grantor with your slightest question.
4. Respond to all grantor issues.
5. Do not disregard a topic.
6. Use the grantor's order for parts of the proposal.
7. Use the grantor's name for parts of the proposal.
8. Never fail to return a form.
9. Never return a form blank.
10. Write simply—Hemingway not Faulkner.
11. "No" means "not now."
12. When a proposal fails, get the reader's comments, rewrite, and resubmit.

## *Conclusion*

So there it is, the philosophies and the rules. What remains to be said? Words of encouragement might be appropriate. The project grants process, by its nature, is most competitive. To be successful, one must fail a lot. In fact, the most successful grantseekers are those that fail the most. All that means is that they try the most. This is a game, like any other, that you must play to learn. If you wait until you know what you are doing before you venture into grantseeking, you will never submit a single proposal. The single most important thing that you can do to become a successful grantseeker is to do it, not plan to do it, not take classes and workshops, not read, not practice, but do it. Does that mean that you will submit a bunch of bad proposals? Yes, you probably will, but in the process you will learn and you will improve. Also, it will take time. Give yourself a minimum of two years. Submit a proposal every two months for two years. Every time you fail, request the reader's comments from the grantor, rewrite the proposal based on the reader's comments, and resubmit. Ask the grantor why you failed. Show that you are in the "game" for the long haul. Keep at it. Never give up.

Do these things, while constantly reading and learning, and in two years' time, you will join the club of successful grantseekers, those who fail only six times out of ten. Here is a field in which you can fail much more than you succeed and still be considered a great success.

# Language Tools—
# Quick Reference

## *Wording Tools*

### *Simplify to Clarify*

In writing proposals, it is extremely important to limit or eliminate jargon and to describe your project clearly and concisely. Wordiness must be avoided. Following are some common phrases that should be simplified to avoid excess verbiage.

| **Instead of ...** | **Write ...** |
| --- | --- |
| in view of | because |
| in a number of cases | some or several |
| in the nature of | like or similar to |
| in view of the fact that | because |
| in view of | because |
| in order to | to |
| in the majority of instances | usually or most of |
| in all probability | probably |
| for the purpose of | to |
| have a preference for | prefer |
| with the exception of | except |
| in excess of | more than |
| in the near future | soon |
| in the not too distant future | soon |
| in addition to | also |
| at this point in time | now |
| at the present time | now |
| in the event that | if |
| in the course of | while or during |
| in the vicinity of | near |
| it would thus appear | apparently |
| it is possible that the cause of | the cause may be |
| it is imperative that | be sure that |

| Instead of . . . | Write . . . |
|---|---|
| may result in | may |
| on a few occasions | occasionally |
| in the neighborhood of | about |
| on the other hand | or |
| on the assumption that | assuming that |
| in the amount of | for |
| it may be of interest that | note |
| arrived at the conclusion | concluded |
| make decisions | decide |
| take action | act |
| give assistance to | assist, help |
| last but not least | finally |

Resort to purple rose—words found only in unabridged dictionaries (and even then often archaic terms no longer in popular usage), banalities, pompous verbal posing, and relatively unknown words used where simpler words would do—is bad writing.

> *The Consultant's Guide to Proposal Writing*
> Written by Herman Holtz
> Published by John Wiley & Sons, Inc.

Proposals that ramble, are filled with jargon and $5 words, and contain sentences with obscure meanings are a dead giveaway that the writer does not have a great deal to say. Successful proposals are written about concrete, well-developed projects, not vague (however good) ideas. When a writer resorts to flowery, bureaucratic language, it is almost always because the writer does not have a clear picture of the project about which he or she is writing. The pompous language sounds good to the ear, and it can fool the casual reader. The experienced reviewer will analyze the writing for its meaning. The reviewer does not have time to play games. He or she cannot spend hours translating difficult prose to see if you, in fact, have met all the requisite criteria for an award. Do not cover up a lack of knowledge with pontification.

### Proposal Writing Tips

- Thoroughly develop the project about which you are writing. Work out all the details before you put pen to paper or fingers to keyboard to write a proposal.
- Develop three outlines from the material supplied by the funder: (1) proposal content requirements, (2) publishing and posting requirements, and (3) potential sales points.

- Develop more outlines. Before you write any part of the proposal, outline your thoughts.

- Do your homework. Research is one of the main components for success in grants acquisition. Back up everything being proposed with precedents, facts and details. You are marketing your project to the potential funder.

- Write clear, definite statements using clear, definite words.

- Eliminate jargon. Jargon can be useful when you are communicating with your colleagues; you can transmit volumes of information in a few words. Proposal readers, however, may not be versed in your jargon. Your points may not be made clearly, simply because of a jargon barrier. Use lay language.

- Use complex sentences sparingly and only to avoid making the text sound choppy.

- Rather than put a long list of things in a sentence, make a bulleted list that can be absorbed at a glance.

- Rather than describe a complicated process in sentences and paragraphs, make a chart or a graphic.

- No bureaucrap! Do not say, "one is able to entice an equine quadruped to liquid refreshment, but one cannot require it to quaff." Say, "You can lead a horse to water, but you can't make it drink."

- Write in short paragraphs of three to five sentences each.

- Be very careful only to use pronouns when they clearly reference their respective nouns.

- Have an "outsider" read your proposal to ensure that you are saying what you think you are saying. A sentence may sound perfectly logical to the writer but be unintelligible to the reader!

- The main way to overcome "writer's block" is to have something to say. This is why you must have a fully developed project before you start writing a proposal. It gives you something to write about.

- One way to overcome writer's block is to begin (physically do it—don't think—write, type, or keyboard) writing "about" what you are supposed to be writing. If the topic is birds, you might start something like this, "Well, I have to write a paper on birds. I don't know the first thing about birds, especially seabirds of the Pacific Coast. I'm supposed to tell about their eating habits, their migratory patterns and their mating rituals. Seabirds eat fish, I guess. What else can they eat, oysters? Doesn't seem likely. Do we even have oysters on the West Coast? I know they migrate—birds, I mean, not oysters. Part of the year I don't see those black ones with the orange slash down the side of their neck." Continue to ramble along until you finally "catch," and the topic and its organization begins to make sense to you.

- Splitting an infinitive is not the ultimate transgression it used to be. The sentence "The DA is determined to prosecute vigorously the drug dealer" just doesn't ring as true as "The DA is determined to vigorously prosecute the drug dealer." For infinitives, the days of staying unsplit are numbered. Let your ear be your guide.

- Ending a sentence with a preposition is another venerable old rule that is slowly and deservedly fading away. Winston Churchill said it best after being corrected by an aide for the prepositional trespass. Sir Winston is reported to have retorted, "This is the sort of pettifoggery up with which I will not put." Enough said.

### Action Verb List

In writing a proposal, it is important to keep your wording proactive rather than passive. You want the reader to know that you intend to actively pursue positive results. After writing a number of pages, it gets harder and harder to think of new action words to describe your project activities or compose goal statements. On the following pages are lots of action verbs to help you add variety as well as accuracy to your sentences.

| | | |
|---|---|---|
| accelerate | access | accentuate |
| accomplish | achieve | acquire |
| add | adjust | advertise |
| advise | alleviate | amend |
| amplify | analyze | arrange |
| articulate | ask | assimilate |
| authorize | | |
| | | |
| beat | begin | bring off |
| build | | |
| | | |
| call | cancel | canvas |
| carry out | categorize | check |
| choose | circumvent | classify |
| close | collaborate | collect |
| come | commend | communicate |
| compare | compose | condense |
| conduct | confirm | construct |
| consult | continue | contribute |
| coordinate | cooperate | count |
| create | cultivate | cut |

| | | |
|---|---|---|
| decide | dedicate | define |
| delegate | delay | demonstrate |
| depict | describe | design |
| detail | determine | develop |
| devise | devote | differentiate |
| direct | discontinue | dispatch |
| distribute | divide | do |
| donate | draft | duplicate |

| | | |
|---|---|---|
| earmark | earn | establish |
| evaluate | examine | exceed |
| exempt | expand | extract |

| | | |
|---|---|---|
| find | finish | form |
| formulate | format | fulfill |
| fund | | |

| | | |
|---|---|---|
| generate | get | give |
| go | grade | guide |

| | |
|---|---|
| heighten | help |

| | | |
|---|---|---|
| illustrate | implement | increase |
| incorporate | incur | index |
| indicate | individualize | inform |
| install | institute | instruct |
| interpret | interview | introduce |
| investigate | invent | invite |
| involve | identify | |

| | | |
|---|---|---|
| label | lengthen | lessen |
| limit | link | list |

| | | |
|---|---|---|
| magnify | make | manufacture |
| master | maximize | measure |
| merchandise | merge | mesh |
| mediate | minimize | mix |
| model | modernize | monitor |
| move | | |

| | | |
|---|---|---|
| net | nominate | note |
| nullify | | |

| obey | obligate | offer |
| omit | open | operate |
| oppose | order | organize |
| orient | orientate | |

| package | pass | patent |
| pay | perfect | perform |
| perpetuate | persuade | phase in |
| phase out | pick | place |
| plan | poll | practice |
| prescribe | preserve | price |
| print | process | procure |
| produce | program | project |
| promote | propose | prove |
| provide | publish | publicize |
| purchase | | |

| qualify | quantify | |

| raise | rank | rate |
| read | rebut | record |
| recover | reduce | refine |
| register | relate | remove |
| renovate | repair | replace |
| report | reproduce | request |
| research | require | reserve |
| resolve | respond | restore |
| restrict | retain | reward |

| select | sell | send |
| separate | set up | sort |
| specify | submit | synthesize |
| systematize | | |

| take | teach | test |
| track | trade | train |
| transcribe | transfer | transport |

| use | | |

| verify | | |

| write | | |

# About the Disk

## Contents

| Title | File Name |
|---|---|
| Project Summary—Worksheet | 1303.DOC |
| Goals—Worksheets | 1304.DOC |

**Chapter 14**

| | |
|---|---|
| Dissemination Plan—Worksheet | 1401.DOC |
| Evaluation Plan—Worksheet | 1402.DOC |
| Continuation Plan—Worksheet | 1403.DOC |
| Management Plan—Worksheet | 1404.DOC |
| Time Lines—Worksheet | 1405.DOC |
| Key Personnel—Worksheet | 1406.DOC |

**Chapter 15**

| | |
|---|---|
| Budget—Worksheet | 1501.DOC |

**Chapter 17**

| | |
|---|---|
| Cover Letter—Worksheet | 1701.DOC |
| Title Page—Worksheet | 1702.DOC |
| Table of Contents—Worksheet | 1703.DOC |
| Executive Summary—Worksheet | 1704.DOC |
| Introduction—Worksheet | 1705.DOC |

**Chapter 18**

| | |
|---|---|
| Proposal Checklist | 1801.DOC |
| Publishing Checklist | 1802.DOC |
| Packaging and Posting Checklist | 1803.DOC |

## Introduction

The forms on the enclosed disk are saved in Microsoft Word for Windows version 6.0. In order to use the forms, you will need to have word processing software capable of reading Microsoft Word for Windows version 6.0 files.

## System Requirements

- IBM PC or compatible computer
- 3.5" floppy disk drive
- Windows 3.1 or higher

- Microsoft Word for Windows version 6.0 or later or other word processing software capable of reading Microsoft Word for Windows 6.0 files.

  NOTE: Many popular word processing programs are capable of reading Microsoft Word for Windows 6.0 files. However, users should be aware that a slight amount of formatting might be lost when using a program other than Microsoft Word. See readme text file on the disk for more information.

# How to Install the Files onto Your Computer

If you would like to copy the files from the floppy disk to your hard drive, run the installation program by following the instructions below. Running the installation program will copy the files to your hard drive in the default directory C:\NEWFORMS. To install files, do the following:

1. Insert the enclosed disk into the floppy disk drive of your computer.
2. Windows 3.1: From the Program Manager, choose File, Run.
   Windows 95: From the Start Menu, choose Run.
3. Type **A:\SETUP** and press Enter.
4. The opening screen of the installation program will appear. Press Enter to continue.
5. The default destination directory is C:\NEWFORMS. If you wish to change the default destination, you may do so now. Follow the instructions on the screen.
6. The installation program will copy all files to your hard drive in the C:\NEWFORMS or user-designated directory.

# Using the Files

### Loading Files

To use the word processing files, launch your word processing program (e.g., Microsoft Word or WordPerfect). Select File, Open from the pull-down menu. Select the appropriate drive and directory. If you installed the files to the default directory, the files will be located in the C:\NEWFORMS directory. A list of files should appear. If you do not see a list of files in the directory, you need to select WORD DOCUMENT (*.DOC) under Files of Type. Double click on the file you want to open.

Edit the form according to your needs. Note that some files contain multiple forms. You might need to scroll through a file to find the form you need.

### Printing Files

If you want to print the files, select File, Print from the pull-down menu.

### Saving Files

When you have finished editing a file, you should save it under a new file name before exiting your program.

## User Assistance

If you need basic assistance with installation or if you have a damaged disk, please contact Wiley Technical Support at:

Phone: (212) 850–6753
Fax: (212) 850–6800 (Attention: Wiley Technical Support)
Email: techhelp@wiley.com

To place additional orders or to request information about other Wiley products, please call (800) 225–5945.

# Index